VERA M. HUGHES

VERAMARYKIN

A Council House Kid in the 1930s and 40s

Matador
9 Priory Business Park
Kibworth Beauchamp
Leicestershire LE8 0RX, UK
Tel: (+44) 116 279 2299
Fax: (+44) 116 279 2277
Email: books@troubador.co.uk
Web: www.troubador.co.uk/matador

ISBN 978 1780885 346

British Library Cataloguing in Publication Data.
A catalogue record for this book is available from the British Library.

Typeset in 12pt Bembo by Troubador Publishing Ltd, Leicester, UK
Printed and bound in the UK by TJ International, Padstow, Cornwall

Matador is an imprint of Troubador Publishing Ltd

Special thanks to Peter my son for his support, encouragement and technical expertise

INTRODUCTION

Four million new houses were built in the 1920s and 30s, partly to further David Lloyd George's 1918 election pledge "to make Britain a fit country for heroes to live in", but also to alleviate the decline in privately rented accommodation caused by government controlled restrictions. In large cities slum clearances were also underway. Women's views were sought for the plans for Local Council Rented Housing and these included the demands for extra bedrooms, indoor lavatories, separate parlours, and gardens. For working class families home ownership was largely seen as unattainable through cost, and privately rented houses were mostly also unaffordable, so that houses in the new Council Housing Estates were eagerly sought by those living in overcrowded and poor conditions. These Estates were often reckoned by the loftier heights of the middle classes as only one small step up from the slums, and vandalism, public drunkenness and riotous behaviour was expected, with gangs of uncontrollable children roaming the streets. None of this was rife in our experience of life in the first quarter century of the Downham Estate. But the slur was, I felt, always there, and outside the Estate one never confessed to being a "council house kid". For those of us in SE London there were no heavy industries nearby and the majority of the householders on the Downham Estate were "white collar" rather than "manual" working class. Mothers stayed at home, and with no help in the home the daily chores of housework, shopping, laundry, child care, etc. provided them with fulltime work in the house. Perhaps my childhood memories may help to redefine the life of families like mine in these large purpose-built estates, whose ambitions were modest and where achievements in terms of forming happy, hard-working families should not be underestimated.

This history of my childhood lays no claim to being a definitive picture of life in the 30's and 40's, and is certainly not meant to be a detailed and all embracing family history: others in the family have researched this with different aims. My aim is to present my life as it appeared to me then and I am very conscious of the very small pond in which I swam.

I have no diary of events with which to refresh or date my recollections and I have therefore no means of putting them in chronological order, but I have tried to show through these anecdotes and family photos my progression through early childhood, adolescence and the beginning of adulthood, when I left school in 1945 and took my place in the world as a wage earner. Very little of the world outside my home impinged on my years as a child and the upheaval of life in wartime had simply to be accepted and endured. It is said that what you have never had you never miss and that was certainly true of the constricted life we all led as adolescents. No gradual awakening of cultural awareness through theatre or other arts was possible for us, and life outside our own little community was largely an unknown factor.

My position as youngest of my parents' two children with a gap of almost four and a half years between my elder brother and me precluded, I now believe, my being fully conversant with family plans, problems, decisions or relationships. Information came to me on a 'need to know' basis and as children at that time were not encouraged to question their elders, this partly explains my occasional impressions of being lost in an adult world. These impressions do not augur well for personal confidence in adult life, a life that is outside the remit of this memoir.

I have tried to avoid too much history that I could not have known at the time, but the backgrounds of some close family members colours their reactions to me and mine to them, and the fuller accounts I give of some of my parents' relatives are facts I learnt about them much later in life and flesh out their characters. It is tempting to go on to describe 'what happened next' to those closest to me, but that is not the purpose of these memoirs.

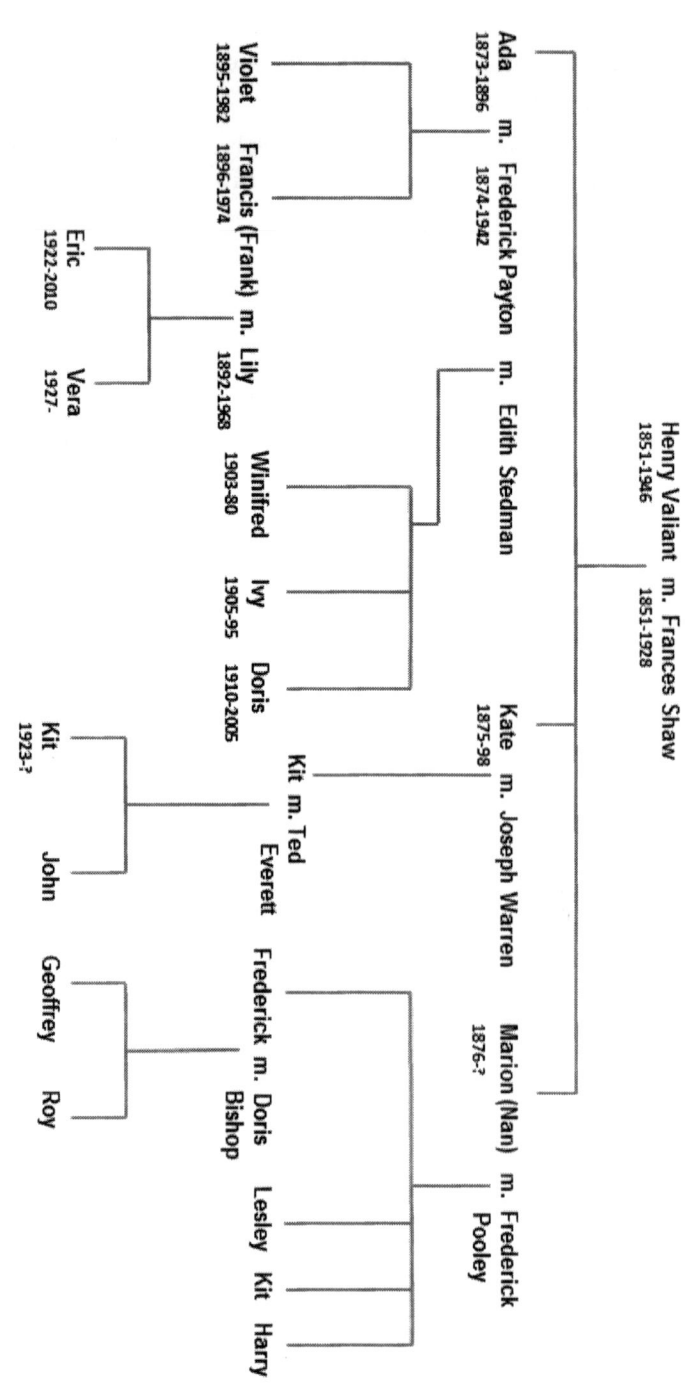

Henry Valliant m. Frances Shaw
1851-1946   1851-1928

Ada   m.   Frederick Payton
1873-1896   1874-1942

Violet   Francis (Frank) m. Lily
1895-1982   1896-1974   1892-1968

Eric   Vera
1922-2010   1927-

m. Edith Stedman

Winifred   Ivy   Doris
1903-80   1905-95   1910-2005

Kate   m. Joseph Warren
1875-98

Kit m. Ted
Everett

Kit   John
1923-?

Marion (Nan)   m. Frederick
1876-?   Pooley

Frederick m. Doris
Bishop

Geoffrey   Roy

Lesley   Kit   Harry

CHAPTER ONE

The Valiant family – The Paytons – meeting Lily –
Frank and Lily's marriage

Where to begin? A good starting place would seem to be with the oldest member of the family that I can remember. He was Henry Valiant, my Great Grandfather, who was born in 1851 and lived to be 95 years old. He was a benevolent presence, sending Christmas presents to Eric and I when we were very young, and I saw him once when he was in his nineties and living on his own in a bed-sitting room, mending a watch which he had in pieces before him on the table.

Henry and his wife Frances had three daughters, Ada, Kate and Marion, all of whom married and bore children. Sadly, Ada and Kate both died in their early twenties. Ada's eldest child Violet was taken in by her maternal grandparents and Francis (Frank) my father, who was only a few months old when his mother died, was absorbed into the Valiant household. It was a second family for Henry and Frances in their forties as they also brought up Kate's daughter Kit Warren and an orphaned niece Ellen Shaw (Nell). The third daughter Marion (Nan) married Frederick Pooley and had four children.

Ada Valiant had married Frederick James Payton, the son of a grocer with his own shop, and after eight years of lonely widowhood Frederick married his second wife Edith Stedman.

Henry Valiant with his grandson Francis Frederick Payton

Grandpa and Grandma Valiant with niece Nell and granddaughter Kit

It was decided that Violet and Frank should not suffer the upheaval of removal from their grandparents' homes, and Frederick and Edith soon produced their own family: three daughters, Winifred Edith, born in 1904, with Ivy Dorothy following in 1905 and Doris (Dorrie) being born in 1910.

On leaving school my father Frank became employed by a large grocery business, Spears and Ponds, but in October 1914, being then eighteen and four months old, he volunteered and

Win, Dorrie and Ivy

was called for military service – no doubt with all the enthusiasm of a young man seeking adventure in a world of men. A family story told to me related that after basic training he was sent to France early in 1915. No doubt letters home revealed his vague but French location which alerted his Grandmother to action. It seems that promises had been made by the War Office in 1914 not to send men to France under the age of nineteen years, and I have read other confirmatory evidence of this. It is possible that Frank lied about his age, or a mistake had been made, but Frances took action by writing to his commanding officer through his regiment and he was returned to England promptly. This may have been a lifesaver as casualty figures were high in the Battle of Ypres in 1915. In common with many veterans of the war, Frank never spoke of his experiences, but his official Army records show that he served in France, Egypt, Gallipoli and Malta, was wounded twice, and gassed in 1918. What a survivor!

Frank's Aunt Nan had married Fred Pooley and their home in Bellingham in SE London became a focus for the younger members of the family. They enjoyed holding large family

Frank, aged 21, on leave in 1917

5

parties and at one of these when he was on leave in the latter half of the Great War, Frank met Lily May Smith who, it was said, accidentally spilt his beer over him. Lily was a friend of Kit Warren, his cousin, and they were both employed in a factory on Shooters Hill, Blackheath, cutting out Army uniforms with huge knives in slots on tables.

Lily May Smith

In her late twenties toward the end of the war, Lily had not expected to get married: the previous four years having carried off so many suitable young men, and she probably saw her life as permanent housekeeper for her father. But Frank, after their courtship, and her junior by four years, proposed to and married serious-eyed, auburn-haired Lily, said later by a former classmate to have been at school "the prettiest girl in Catford".

The wedding photo of Frank and Lily

Lily, Wagg, Frank and Vic in party mood, December 1924

Lily was the eldest daughter of Charles Smith, a self-employed painter and decorator. Her elder brother, also Charles, was always known as Wagg, and was somewhat disabled by curvature of the spine incurred, so family legend had it, after he had fallen downstairs as a child but had not been examined by a doctor for possible injury. There were three other children in the family: Florence (Flo), Ernest, and Victor Lionel, at whose birth his mother died. Lily was eleven years old at the time, and although her father attempted to employ housekeepers, none stayed for very long, and when Lily left school at fourteen she was obliged to take on the running of the household and the upbringing of Victor, then aged three. This forged a strong bond of affection between Lily and Vic, and when I was a child Uncle Vic visited us almost weekly and was a firm favourite with children, especially at our birthday parties. Lily's sister Flo married Percy Havers and left home as soon as she could. Eric, my brother, had a story that Ernest joined the Army as soon as possible to avoid the attention of the police, for some unknown misdemeanour.

Sadly, Ernest was killed in France and no known grave or information was kept regarding his life or death.

Lily became the mainstay of the family. She once told me of helping in her father's business when she was quite young by sitting atop a step ladder in a client's house trimming lengths of wallpaper for her father to paste and hang. At that time wallpaper was made with a half-inch plain border down each side. To hang it one edge had to be trimmed off and abutted and overlapped on the piece already in place on the wall — it seems that even then she had skilful fingers.

CHAPTER TWO

The life-saver – Audrey – a new baby – the new house –
the Estate – a full-sized bed – my dolls and Teddy

Frank and Lily spent their early married life as tenants in the top rooms of a house in Peak Hill Gardens in Sydenham. Frank's cousin Kit Warren had married Edward (Ted) Everett and they lived downstairs in the same house. Lily must have welcomed the change to a smaller household to care for when Eric Frank Ernest was born late in 1922. His life might have been cut short at about eighteen months but for the quick thinking of a neighbour called in by Lily in great distress. Eric was suffering a killer disease of the time, Whooping Cough, and was wheezing and desperately trying to breathe. The neighbour, no doubt drawing on experience immediately upended the baby, holding him head down by his feet as the mucus drained out of his lungs, saving his life. My mother did her best to build up Eric's strength after this illness with careful feeding and even though they could not afford it for themselves, she bought two ounces of butter a week especially for Eric.

Milk at that time was delivered by horse and cart, with the customer having to go out into the road to have the milk scooped out of the churn and poured into the customer's own jug. My mother, to avoid being given short measure bought a measuring jug of her own which ensured she bought full pints and received full value for money which was not at all plentiful then. My parents were advised that sea air would be beneficial and they somehow managed to pay for a three-week stay by the sea for Eric and Lil.

Cousin Kit and Ted Everett produced a daughter, Audrey, and the two children were company for each other. Grandpa Valiant had made Eric a book, foolscap size, by cutting out, assembling on pages and carefully painting the new Rupert adventures by Mary Tourtell published by the Daily Express. One day Eric and Audrey were sitting side by side on the stairs, both about three or four with the book spread over their knees. A neighbour could hear Eric's voice and asked his mother incredulously "Can he read?" "Oh no," said Lily, "he's reading the pictures!" Repeatedly listening to the stories had made him word-perfect!

Eric at the seaside aged 1 ¾ years

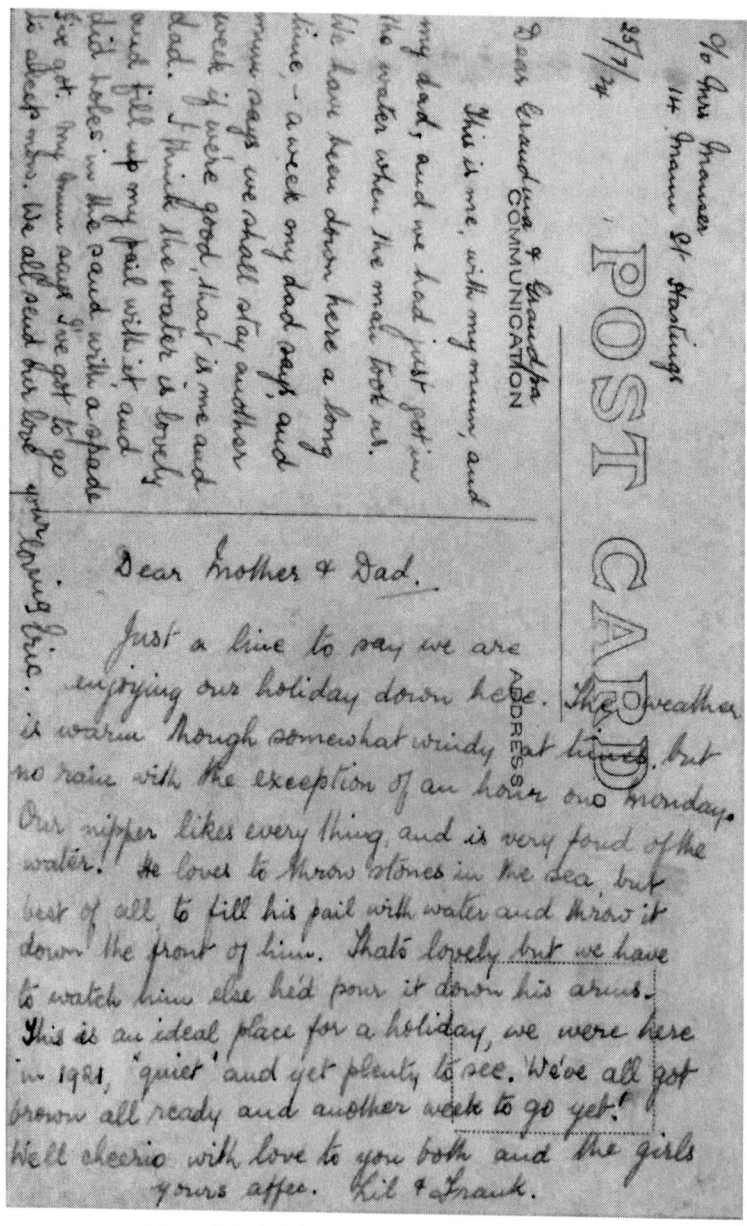

News of the holiday on the reverse of previous photo

In due course when Eric was three and a half, Lily found herself pregnant again. When in the following spring she decided the birth was imminent she hauled herself at 8.30am on to a tram and alighted at a Nursing Home in Rushey Green, Catford, and I was born at noon on March 16th 1927. All went well at my birth, but Lily developed phlebitis in her leg. Part of the treatment in those days involved lying flat in bed with sandbags along the sides of the legs to prevent movement. The whole treatment for the condition took six weeks. Once more the family came to Frank's rescue and this time it was Eric who was sent away from home to live temporarily with his Grandparents and "the girls" (Win, Ivy and Dorrie) who were now in their twenties, – "flappers" perhaps?

Although Eric was much loved and every care was taken of him in his grandmother's home, he must have felt the absence of his mother for six weeks as a traumatic experience. No doubt Frank visited his father, stepmother and stepsisters as often as he could, but the upheaval for Eric must have been great. Then, when he returned home at last to his parents there was a new baby to accommodate, and Eric was no longer the absolute centre of his parents' lives. The effect of these experiences on a four year old child cannot be accurately judged, but it may be significant that Eric developed a stammer which troubled him into adulthood. Perhaps, too, there was some lingering, hidden resentment towards the baby who had usurped his position in the family.

Lily, Vera and Eric on holiday at Westcliff 1928

My parents found life with two children, their "pigeon pair", aged four and one year, very cramped in their flat, especially when both of us became infected with Chicken Pox, and they applied to the Borough Council for a house on one of the new estates that were springing up in the suburbs. "The man from the Council" duly visited to check their eligibility for a place on the list and they showed him how cramped for room they were. My Father's war service and the fact that he was in steady employment must have backed-up their case, and in 1929 they were allocated a two-bedroomed house, one of the "Homes fit for Heroes" on the "green fields of Downham", erected and managed by the London County Council although the address was "Downham, Bromley, Kent".

The Downham Estate was built on farmland and the farm

name was retained in "Shroffold" Road which ran through the centre of the estate. Verdant Lane from Catford ran past Hither Green Cemetery to become Northover, crossing Shroffold Road and continuing up the hill to become Southover on its way to Bromley. The estate was roughly circular in shape and as well as Roundtable Road, a horseshoe shape, most of the new roads were given the names of Knights of the Roundtable, e.g., Ballamore, Bedivere, Gareth, Lamerock, Launcelot, and Tristram. Merlin made the Round Table for Uther Pendragon and Vanoc was Merlin's young son: Merlin and Vanoc both lent their names to small closes or Gardens. Camlan Road is named after the battle of Camlan in Cornwall where Arthur is reputed to have received his death wound, putting an end to the Knights of the Roundtable.

There were two Infants and Junior Schools on the estate – Pendragon and Ballamore – rivals in some ways. A third school on Durham Hill was the local Senior School for those who did not qualify for either a Grammar or Central School place after the age of eleven. A Public House, The Northover, was later built at the junction of Verdant Lane and Northover. It was painted a blinding white which after the outbreak of war was obliterated with green and brown camouflage paint. The row of poor shed-like stalls in the lane were rebuilt as small shops to serve the surrounding area. The land is hilly and the road from there, Northover, rises to the junction with Shroffold Road, where the church, St. Luke's, was erected, and rises again to meet Downham Way where there was a row of shops and a public house, The Tavern.

Before I graduated to a single-size bed I was once left in my cot in the bedroom nearer the fireplace, under the charge of my father who was working in the garden: I was recovering from measles. To keep me amused I had been given a newspaper and some safe scissors "to cut out the pictures". Looking at the pictures, sitting up with crossed legs, my right elbow resting on my knee and my head resting on the hand with the scissors, I was amazed to find pieces of hair falling on the paper. Hastily gathering them up, I stuffed them under the pillow to make them go away. My mother later told of her surprise at finding fluffy hair on the floor under the cot and a lop-sided daughter. She said she had to cut the hair on the left side of my centre parting to match the right side – I must have looked rather odd.

I was taken around in a pushchair that remains in the memory simply as a large black hole (the hood), into which one climbed. Similarly the brown varnished highchair is remembered simply as rather treacherous when it was being swivelled down to make a low chair with table, as it had a small cogged wheel on the side which could painfully trap little fingers when in action.

Family on the beach at Herne Bay in 1929

The house we were allocated was in the centre of a block of eight on Northover, with Durham Hill and Lamerock Road running up each side. The front garden consisted mainly of a grass bank with five steps up to a shared porch, and the slope was repeated in the back garden where a strip of asphalt gave way to four steps leading up to the garden. The two main rooms downstairs both had coal fires, one with a bread oven over. Both needed black-leading. The two rooms could be opened into one by pulling back the folding doors between them. In the winter we tended to live in the front room which was smaller and cosier, with half the folding doors closed and all covered by long blue curtains. The door from this room to the passage was usually blocked off by furniture, so the exit was via the dark dash behind the curtain into the back room and immediately out into the passage. It always seemed like a celebration of summer when the folding doors were fully opened and the furniture re-arranged so that a large room was formed from the front to the back of the house. When I was very small, Eric sometimes sat me on an old curtain and gave me 'sledge' rides the length of the room on the polished lino. Turning at the end added to the excitement, especially if I fell off!

The kitchen, always called the 'scullery', was a narrow room with no space for a table, but the table top of the large mangle made a work-top when required for cooking purposes. The walls were of unplastered brick, white-washed or distempered white. The scullery was equipped with a large wooden dresser with cupboards top and bottom and a drawer between. On the same side as the dresser was a gas cooker, and on the opposite wall a deep sink and wooden dish-draining board. A high shelf ran on both sides of the room and a wash boiler stood between the sink and the door to the back garden. The fire under the boiler had to be lit and fed with coal or coke to boil white clothes and sheets on wash-days and to provide hot water for baths. This was easily transferred upstairs to the bathroom by a fixed hand-pump over the boiler.

The scullery was at one end of the passage and at the other end was the front door alongside the larder from where, it was said, it was possible to eavesdrop on any conversation carried on outside in the porch! Hanging inside the larder was a brown paper carrier bag into which coupons and tokens from various groceries were saved and redeemed when sufficient. That was probably how I acquired my Sunny Jim doll. Packets of 'Force', the original toasted corn flakes, would have had coupons to redeem for a replica soft toy about ten inches tall. The slogan "High o'er the fence leaps Sunny Jim, Force is the food that raises him!", was often repeated as an advertising rhyme. In the passage was also the door to the coal cellar under the stairs, which had front boards slotted in according to the amount of coal within.

Upstairs there were two bedrooms and a bathroom with a lavatory. In the corner of my parents' bedroom was a space with its own window, where my cot was placed, and it was just large enough for a single bed for me later. Eric, of course, was given the smaller bedroom, where I rarely set foot and was not welcomed.

Alongside the end of my bed when installed and parallel to it there was just room for my dolls' cot. This had been made by my parents; my father constructing the framework of a rectangular bed about eight inches deep on struts in a folding deck-chair form. There was also a canopy supported by a single upright at one end with a top bar extending part-way over the cot, from which side curtains hung. My mother made all the bedding, the bed, and the lace-trimmed canopy, and it was large enough to hold all my dolls. These, in the order of seniority were Mary whose porcelain head had unfortunately suffered a severe haircut in her youth and who was obliged always to wear her brown velvet fur-trimmed bonnet and matching coat with fur-trimmed collar. Next was Topsy. She was brown all over, with only painted hair, yellow clothes and not much personality. Then later along came Wendy. She was a red plush floppy type of doll with a large face and long limbs. There was room too for my golliwog and Sunny Jim. Much later I had a small 'baby' doll, but by far the most handled and loved toy was my Teddy. In the style of the time he had a pointed nose, which became rather threadbare, and his paws and soles of his feet at some time were re-covered with brown velvet. He sported a smart blue jumper and short trousers, knitted by my mother, as were all the dolls' clothes. As I snuggled down in bed on my right side with my knees bent, he would sit on my lap with his head under my chin as I dropped off to sleep, in the winter with the warmth of a stone hot water bottle in its knitted cover near my feet. I do not remember carrying him about, but he certainly featured in my games with the dolls, and also rode in the dolls' pram. I have no memory of relinquishing these much-loved toys, but I rather think they were given away by my mother during the war.

Although I did not have a real speech defect, it was noticed that I had trouble in pronouncing the letter R at the beginning of words and it was thought a little careful practice in speaking it would help. So I was rehearsed in a sentence which I tried to master. My parents must have suppressed some amusement as with huge concentration I clearly stated: " Wound the wagged wocks the wagged wascal wan". The difficulty faded with age, but I never have learned how to roll those R's!

CHAPTER THREE

Grandad to stay – the Baker Street shop – cinema tales – Zoo visit – the Aunties – holidays at the seaside – arcade adventures

My grandad, Charles Smith, came to stay with us for some months in 1930. He must have been in his early sixties then and perhaps for some reason was temporarily without a home. A bed was put up for him in the downstairs front room and I used to enjoy helping my mother fluff up the feather mattress, which seemed a great luxury to me, and make the bed each morning. He played simple quiet games with me, and if we had one he would upend a little sweet bag on the coal shovel, light the two top corners and hold it in the fireplace, when the hot air would waft the bag in flames up the chimney to my great delight.

Lily with her father Charles Smith in the garden in Northover

I believe my Father probably rejoined Spears and Ponds after he was demobilised, but needing a position with better prospects he became employed by Messrs Keith Prowse. It may be that Uncle Fred Pooley helped him to find this position as I understand that Uncle Fred was connected to music publishing as a storekeeper. Keith Prowse were music publishers, also selling gramophones and records and some small musical instruments. They also made bookings for foreign holidays and travel and did much business in theatre seat booking. Frank progressed fairly rapidly and became the Manager of one of their smaller shops in Baker Street. This was a kind of "half-shop" with one shop window, one door, a small area with a counter for theatre and travel tickets, and stairs down to a basement which held another counter, the sheet music department, gramophones, records and small instruments. There were two small cubicles for customers to listen to records before purchasing them, and a small area behind them with a sink and a gas ring. I never heard of any assistant being employed, but there was a porter who swept up and kept the shop front clean and polished. On one or two very rare visits Eric and I delighted in tidying up the brochures and leaflets on the counters, causing my father to say afterwards that he couldn't find anything he needed!

My mother was the linchpin of the family. While my father worked hard and also cultivated the garden, my mother turned the house into a home. She had had much housekeeping experience before and since her marriage but it must have been far more rewarding to organise her own home. Lily saw to it that Frank was always well turned out for work. The breadwinner was seen off to catch the train to Charing Cross Station each morning with his bowler hat well brushed, his suit smart and his boots well-polished. Frayed shirt collars and cuffs were expertly turned to give them new life and pieces of the tail were used if necessary.

The shirts were only ever bought cheaply in the Sales where good quality shirts were considerably reduced in price and could be found in Department Stores. My parents worked out a good system where a new suit, in the middle range of prices, was bought every nine months, so that Frank always looked smart as a Shop Manager. His cast-off, but not too-worn suits were often shortened in the sleeves and legs to fit Wagg, who eked out a living on his own as a painter and decorator. I am sure he was grateful for Lily's work and these handouts, and also for the welcome and good meals he enjoyed on his visits to us. He was pleasant and quiet but had no real interest in Eric and me.

My father took his lunch to work each day in a brown varnished plywood box he had made which accommodated two pudding basins side by side in compartments. One basin would contain a serving of the previous day's main meal, and the other a portion of pudding or pie. He was fond of desserts and often had two helpings at home. The basins were heated up in turn in a saucepan of water over the gas ring in the shop – child's play for one who had lived in the trenches for four years! In this way he was provided with a hot meal daily without the trouble and expense of finding a café or restaurant.

When I was very small and Eric about seven we were taken to the cinema, the Splendid in Bromley Road, to see "Rin Tin Tin", who was the forerunner of "Lassie – the Wonderdog" of later fame. Rin Tin Tin was a wonderful alsatian dog who bounded about the screen performing spectacular and incredible rescues and foiling nefarious criminals. All very exciting, and enhanced for everyone, I am sure, by my cries of "Bow-wow, bow-wow" every time he filled the screen. The next cinema visit, probably a year or so later was less enjoyable, for me, anyway. We probably went as a treat for Eric as it was an African adventure story. All the white men were suntanned in shorts and white pith helmets, while hordes of dancing, painted Africans wielded spears. I sat on my mother's lap, but the sight of a grimacing, painted brown face enlarged to fill the screen as it came towards us was enough to make me scream in terror. It was said afterwards that I never liked ugly faces, which was proved later on a visit in about 1937 to see "Lost Horizon". The sight of the young heroine's face as she left the magical valley of Shangri-la, ageing two hundred years in only a few minutes filled me with horror. The round face covered with wrinkles and unrecognisable as the young girl haunted my dreams and nightmares for at least a year. I was not too happy about the face of the evil Queen in Snow White either. At least my Shangri-la nightmare was about something I had seen, and it replaced an earlier nightmare horror of a witch, tall and dressed in black with a pointed hat. The particular awfulness about her was that on her feet she wore a kind of snowshoes which protruded back and front. I would see the back extensions of these shoes poking towards me under a door and knew she was the other side of it, just waiting. I learnt how to break the nightmare by licking my fingers and rubbing them across my eyelids, and it always worked. Where do these childhood fantasies come from?

While I was still small enough to be carried by my father we had a day at the London Zoo. We saw the penguins in their splendidly modernistic pool with sloping walkways, and the polar bears on their Mappin Terraces and then went to see the monkeys. My father held me up close to the cage to offer the monkey a peanut in its shell. The monkey made a quick grab, took the peanut and my finger with it, which was scratched by its long nails. The Keeper was called and he very kindly took us behind the cages where my finger was bathed and tears stopped. No fuss, no anti-tetanus injection, no forms to sign, no insurance claims. What a different era! But I have never really liked monkeys since then. As a treat Eric and I were given a ride on a camel. Why not an elephant ride? Either the queue was too long or the fee too expensive, but the camel was the next best thing. So there we were, sitting astride between the humps, me in front with Eric holding me from behind, while the camel took us for a stately but wobbling walk. I was not too happy with this ride as I was expected to hold on to the camel's hump which I found to be covered with nasty prickly hairs. I much preferred going to see the parrots and then the sealions being fed.

I have no knowledge of my father's relationship with his father, step-mother and stepsisters during their childhood, but from the early 30's I witnessed only affection and loving kindness between them and us. Grandma and 'the Aunties', as we called them, made much of Eric and I.

Win and Ivy as girls had both won scholarships to James Allen School in Dulwich where Grandpa had his grocery shop: Win at age 11 in February 1915 and Ivy at 9-and-a-half three months later won Foundation Scholarships. Their parents presented each of them with an autograph book inscribed in Win's case "From Mum and Dad for obtaining a London County Council scholarship", and in Ivy's inscribed "As a token of appreciation from Mum and Dad for obtaining a James Allen Foundation Scholarship when nine and a half years old." From James Allen School they proceeded to Christ's Hospital, Hertford, a prestigious girls' school. By the early 30s when I first knew them they were in their mid-20's and pursuing very successful secretarial careers. Between 1928 and 1929 Ivy had taken courses at the Regent Street Polytechnic and passed "with merit" in French shorthand and Commercial French and German. By the beginning of the war they both held senior positions in different branches of the paper industry, and both firms were evacuated to Reading, where they had to live in digs. They had enjoyed cycling as young women and had a circle of friends with whom they had holidays abroad. Win became a keen photographer, later entering the Croydon Camera Club's exhibitions with success. Ivy had been a member of Mrs Prunella Stack's League of Health and Beauty in its heyday. They both retired in the early 1960s to Broadstairs in Kent. I know less about Dorrie and no records of her childhood remain. She was some six years younger than Win and perhaps not academically inclined. At the age of 25 she was a Sunday School teacher and also played the piano, and also encouraged my interest in natural history – the caterpillar section. In the early part of the war she left home to train as a nurse and in 1943 she was jointly in charge of a home for young children near Oxford. She later joined an Anglican religious order at Burnham Abbey near Maidenhead where she spent her days as a nun until her death at the age of 95.

Win aged 25

Ivy aged 22

Dorrie aged 20

My parents loved holidays by the sea and perhaps following on from Eric's seaside convalescence after whooping cough they tried to spend my father's annual holiday at a Kentish resort, being not too far away. The trunk would be packed and sent off by rail to our destination and somehow conveyed to our digs. On the morning of our departure, when I was old enough, I would be dressed in my holiday clothes and sent to the Rent Office with a brown paper envelope containing the Rent Book and a fortnight's rent in advance. Great care was taken by cautious tenants not to do anything that could lead to expulsion by the Council and defaulting on the rent had to be avoided at all costs by the prudent tenant.

Margate became a favourite resort as the sand was plentiful and cleaned every day of seaweed and rubbish by lorries with rakes before the arrival of the holidaymakers in the mornings. Ramsgate did not have this beach-cleaning service as a day trip from Margate showed, and our sandcastle digging turned up waste newspaper and other less hygienic scraps. Similarly Broadstairs did not meet parental approval either for a different reason, as they found that the bay seemed to be a heat trap and constricting. So Margate won hands down for several years.

Vera barely suppressing the giggles and Eric exploring the rocks. Margate 1931

On one holiday at Margate we had an arrangement with our landlady that she would cook a main meal for us from food we provided. This meant that our first call of the day was to buy meat and other food and return with it to the house before we could go down to the beach, which was rather a nuisance. As a holiday treat for all of us we often went into a Lyons Teashop for a morning cup of tea, and Eric and I were allowed to choose a cake each. We always had our mother's cakes at home and thought the variety of shop cakes were a treat. Eric always chose a conical madeline covered with coconut with a cherry on the top, and I always chose a chocolate cupcake with its thick sweet chocolate icing on the top. The routine when we arrived on the beach seldom varied from year to year. Having found a suitable sandy place above the high-tide mark Eric and I would dig a shallow squarish pit for our parents to sit in, piling up the sand to make a backrest. A waterproof sheet would be placed in it and there they would sit, Dad smoking his pipe and reading a newspaper, and Mum usually knitting and watching us. Eric and I would build sandcastles and play at the water's edge and sometimes my father would also join our games with a beach ball in the sea. My mother unfortunately could not participate in sand games or paddling as she had to wear thick pink elastic stockings from instep to just below the knee as treatment for the varicose veins she had suffered since my birth and as a preventive from varicose ulcers. The stockings were of necessity difficult to put on and remove on the beach and so she preferred to sit with her legs supported, and the "nest" we made in the sand was better for her than sitting in a deckchair and, of course, saved the deckchair fee.

After a day on the beach and a meal we would usually walk along the promenade and perhaps have an ice-cream or, for me, a Candy Floss. This confection of pink spun sugar on a stick needed careful handling, especially if there was a breeze. Instead of biting into it, which usually left me with sticky strands in my hair, I had to pull pieces off to eat it. Sticky and messy, but so sweet and sugary, it was worth being cleaned up afterwards with hankies and spit! There were plenty of seaside shows on offer, but these were not deemed by my parents as suitable for children, even if funds would stretch that far, but we felt no desire to see them. There were various amusements to watch and one year having watched a "Guess your weight for tuppence" showman for several minutes I was pushed forward as a customer and the tuppenny fee was paid. I stood stolidly mute while he grasped my upper arms and announced "Four Stone Five Pounds." I think he was probably right most of the time, but not about this customer. On his machine I weighed 5 Stone 4 Pounds, and so we got our money back. He wanted to shake hands with me, the customer who had beaten him, but as I was clutching several liquorice comfits which had bled their colours on to my sticky palm I could only offer a left hand. I thought I would rather have had a prize!

Every year I yearned for one of the large blow-up beach toys on sale in Woolworths. As well as huge beach-balls there were, more to my liking, large ducks, fish, or various animals. If I had asked for one, which I probably did not, I felt it would probably have been explained to me that they were not worth the money as they could be used only once a year on holiday, and where would we put it anyway in our luggage? So I made do with my bucket and spade and sand patters my father had made.

We spent most of our days on the beach, only visiting amusement arcades in poor weather. Margate had its famous Dreamland Fun Fair which we explored one rainy day. Eric had some pocket money and tried his luck on "Bunty Pulls the String", a table of prizes, each with a string attached rising to a ceiling about two feet above, and being gathered together in a bunch for the customer to pull an end. I think there were some strings with no prizes or worthless ones, but Eric was lucky and pulled up a small box of chocolates. Great excitement, and after a minute or two he paid for me to have a go, showing me a particular string to pull. It was slightly frayed, I believe. So, hey presto, I won a box of chocolates too! The owners of the stall were not at all pleased but had to give me my prize. As we walked away and looked back they were glaring at us and examining the strings. Then large scissors were produced and all the ends cut off straight. I do not think there were many chocolates left in my box by the end of the evening, but I am sure Eric's box was as new!

Occasionally we visited one of the smaller arcades, little bigger than a room really, with simple "Try your luck" games around and on the walls. On one such visit when I had spent my few pennies I dropped a little silver "thruppenny joey" out of my little purse and although my father and I searched the floor it could not be found and I was very upset as it was more than a week's pocket money. However, the next morning my father insisted that he and I should go and search again and, lo and behold, there was the thruppenny joey leaning up against the skirting board. Hurrah! Hurrah! Whether it was actually the one I had lost that had mysteriously managed to survive there overnight never entered my head. I rather suspect my father's kind heart and sleight of hand had something to do with the discovery. He was very fond of "Polly", or "Pol", as he called me when I was little, and the affection was reciprocated.

CHAPTER FOUR

The tormentor – the M.U. outing – the first garden – to Grandma's
– neighbours – Sunday School – Infants' School –
my Zoo – the loft mishap

There were happy times for me in the pre-school years as I
played with my dolls and toys when Eric was at school, but when
at home he teased and baited me continually as generations of
big brothers have no doubt always done. The difference in our
ages meant that we did not regularly play together, and he would
delight in tormenting me. He would ambush me from the dark
backroom in the winter or, a favourite trick, wrestle me to the
floor, and kneeling astride me with my arms pinioned, he would
threaten me with a spit-ball ever about to drop on to my face. I
would cry "Stop it, stop it !" and grizzle, my mother would call
from the scullery, "What are you doing, Eric?" "No-o-o-othing!"
he would answer all innocence. "But he was going to" I would
weep. I think his torments made sure that when I cried and
whined I would be called "ratty" and scolded for "crying over
nothing". I made a resolution one year on my birthday, probably
my fifth, to be sure not to cry that day as it was said "if you cried
on your birthday you would cry every day for a year" and I
already seemed to cry a lot anyway.

Since early childhood Eric had been a difficult child to feed.
My parents no doubt tried everything they could in line with

32

current thinking, and probably the shaming of having to take his meal into the garden to eat where the neighbours might see his disgrace was the last in all the efforts to persuade him to "eat up". I saw this order in action only once when he had to take his stewed apples and custard into the garden. Perhaps it was the last occasion.

Physical punishments were not used as the occasional threats of them seemed to be sufficient. A short cane was kept on the high shelf in the scullery and the threat would have been to Eric to "fetch the cane". I never saw this implemented. The threat to me for bad behaviour was "a smacked bottom", which again never actually happened. I think that living in a happy, busy household with loving parents and plenty to occupy us, we were not often tempted to break the few rules that must have existed. I saw no gangs of boys roaming the streets intent on mischief, and Eric joined the Scouts as soon as he was eligible, no doubt at my father's prompting, and would have had plenty to occupy him as a "Tenderfoot". Truancy from school was monitored by the "School Board Man". He was represented to us as a kind of ogre who would call on our parents if we were absent from school without "a note". Sightings of an unknown man with a book knocking on doors in the neighbourhood would send a frisson of alarm through even the most regular school attenders – we were sure he was the "Schoo' Bd' Man'!

Our estate was provided with a church, St Luke's, and although they did not attend the services, my parents sometimes attended social events. My mother joined the Mothers' Union and she took me on one of its outings before I started school. This was a visit to the Shredded Wheat factory in Welwyn Garden City. It was a modern factory; a model for its time, and it was pictured on the boxes of Shredded Wheat, a great slab of concrete with rows and rows of windows. My only memory of the visit is seeing the wheat strands being extruded from a machine and being cut off mechanically, making the familiar pillow shapes. I expect we were also given free samples.

My parents, chiefly my father, worked hard on the garden at the back of the house. He made a rockery on the bank up from the asphalt, to the lawn with flowerbeds each side, and a crazy-paving pathway on the left-hand side. He put up trellises along the fences between our and the neighbours' gardens and along the top of the rockery, ending in an archway at the top of four little steps down to the asphalt. Garden plants were bought cheaply in boxes in the market in Catford. My father worked cheerfully and energetically in the garden, quoting humorously one of the slogans of the time "Workers of the world, unite! You have nothing to lose but your chains!" Was that part of the Communist Manifesto?

The well-stocked garden in Northover

My Payton Grandparents, Frederick and Edith, lived in Tyneham Road off Lavender Hill in Battersea when I first knew them. We would run down the hill, and Eric was tall enough to ring the bell beside the cycle repair shop which Frederick had taken on after leaving the grocery business. They lived behind and over the shop with Win, Ivy and Dorrie. I once stayed with them for a few days, and in the large rather dark living room sat on the floor to watch Mrs Mottram, their "daily", as she black-leaded the grate and polished the fender. I was allowed limited play with Dorrie's leftover dolls and particularly coveted one with articulated joints and a Red Ridinghood costume, but it was not offered to me and I could not ask for it. Getting ready for this trip to Grandma I was lifted and sat on the mangle tabletop while my mother made sure my shoes and socks were clean and hair tidy. I wore a dress with small multi-coloured bean-shaped spots on it with a red collar, short-sleeved cuffs and a band round the bottom, made by my mother, probably from short pieces of material bought in the Sales and matched up. My Grandma had some photos taken of me in a photographic studio; in one I am very serious and in the other, beside a bowl of pale yellow artificial roses, I was allowed a slight smile. There was also a visit to Auntie Amy, Grandma's sister, who had made a special dish of junket as appropriate food for a little girl. I had never seen this pallid, sloppy-looking food before; it was not custard, rice, or blancmange which I knew, so I refused to taste it! Sorry, Auntie Amy.

Looking down from the bedroom into the street beside Win I was amazed to see Ivy call to her and throw up a packet of cigarettes, which Win caught. I had not thought that grownups behaved casually like that, but of course these Aunties were only young women in their twenties. A few years later after Ivy had been in the League of Health and Beauty display in Hyde Park she gave me the short circular skirt and triangular scarf in blue sateen, which formed their costume with a white blouse. The skirt and scarf were useful for dressing-up, and the pair of black ballet-type leather pumps, also passed on, I wore indoors for many years until they fell to pieces. Dear Binkie, the tabby cat, was much in evidence on that visit and Dorrie was trying to teach him to count while he sat on the sewing machine table-flap, by gently thumping his tail in repetition. She claimed he could copy the thumps up to the count of four!

Fun with a cartload of dollies at Grandma's

Studio portraits, even with a duck, are serious business

The centre three pairs of houses in our small terrace shared porches and, neighbours willing, these were ideal playing areas for imaginative games. In the end house on the right were the Wheelers, parents and two boys, the younger of whom was about Eric's age. Next to them were Mr and Mrs Dawes with Peter, whom we thought went to a 'posh' school as when we rarely saw him he seemed always to be in a white shirt and long white trousers, carrying a cricket bat. Mr Dawes worked at night and slept by day and children were not really allowed to play in their porch. Their daughter Brenda was about two years younger than me, the third member of our little trio of Norman Batchelor, Brenda Dawes and me. The Batchelors lived next-door to us and the Dawes, with their two children, Edna and Norman. Edna was a little older than Eric and left school at fourteen, and Norman was just about a year younger than me and my great friend in games with Brenda in our porch. On our other side for several years were the Pyefinches. This family was a little larger and noisier with children Eddie, Tim, and Doris. Mr Pyefinch was a bus driver and in about 1935 they moved to buy a house in Ridgeway Drive on a new estate of private houses about a mile away. The next neighbours to occupy the house were a widowed lady Mrs Gauntlet, seemingly elderly (Old Mother Gauntlet!) and unforthcoming, and her blind son who went out each day to his work as a piano tuner. Norman, sometimes Brenda, and I had become used to playing in the front porch and provided we were not too noisy, continued to do so. Our games often had a strong story line and when teatime stopped play for the day Norman would stand at the top of the steps and loudly announce to the world "I declaim this game to be continued!" In my pedantic way, even then, I was convinced he should say either "I claim ———" or "I declare ———". I thought the word 'declaim' was wrong, and probably did not exist, but it made no difference, Norman still "declaimed"!

Next door to the Pyefinches were the Wellers. Mr Weller was disabled in some way, perhaps from a war wound, and did not go out to work. Mrs Weller loved a good gossip and had the odd habit of mouthing the words spoken to her in an almost simultaneous echo, which enhanced any dramatic news, but she was a cheery soul, with all the chatter. They had two sons; Teddie, well into his teens, and Charley, who was often up to some simple mischief. Mr Weller and Teddie made a small toy theatre with curtains and painted scenery, with the actors in cardboard cut-outs being pushed on and off stage by rods. To the delight of local children, particularly the younger ones like me, they would put on a show in their front room with the audience sitting cross-legged on the floor, enthralled. A few sweets provided by Mrs Weller added to the success of the enterprise. I suppose these shows occurred not more than two or three times during those years, but we found it all magical.

I believe my father may have been taken to church by Grandpa Valiant, and he may perhaps have become a choirboy. He became a Boy Scout – more of which later – and would certainly then have been expected to attend church. My mother did not apparently come from a church-going family, but nevertheless we were taught to "say our prayers" before bed. Since my mother had no experience in these matters we were just taught and recited "Gentle Jesus, meek and mild, Look upon a little child. Pity my simplicity, Suffer me to come to Thee." I did not really understand the words but that did not seem to matter.

Before St Luke's church had a Sunday School I was taken by Eric up Durham Hill and over the top, down to St Barnabas' church in Downham Way. This was quite a way for a four year old, so perhaps it did not happen often, but I remember sitting in a hall on a wooden bench, in the front row for 'Sunday School'. When the Sunday School was started in the Large Hall at St Luke's I attended regularly and there was a very good attendance. It was run by the Misses Neale who lived in Northover, further up the hill to 'the top'. The elder Miss Neale was dark-haired and rather stern-looking and her sister was the smiley one who chatted to you as you got your Sunday school card stamped with a little star at the end of the morning. I am quite sure we met on Sunday mornings because I remember the picture on the wall which fascinated me. It portrayed a little family sitting round a kitchen table, father, mother, at least one little girl, and a baby in a cradle on the floor. The door was open. It was a cottage in the country and the garden outside was bathed in sunshine and full of flowers. The father was saying Grace before their meal and it always made me think of going home to my own Sunday dinner with roast potatoes. We learnt several hymns and I was particularly struck by the imagery in "Hills of the North, rejoice" – with its telling descriptions of pagan peoples being brought to Christianity. For a time I also belonged to the King's Messengers, a church organisation which met in the vestry of the Hall on Saturday mornings, but their programme is lost to me now.

During these early years we had one or two visits to a Pantomime, probably at Catford Town Hall. The story lines are long forgotten, but I clearly remember being entranced and bewitched and in love with any animal be it cat, duck, rabbit or other that was inserted, however improbably, into the plot. Of course, they were people in costumes, but I longed to have the animal to stroke and cuddle and as we left the show felt a sense of loss and bereavement which I kept to myself.

We had two slates and chalks at home. Mine was the smaller with a wooden frame around it and the other was square and larger with a rather battered edge, and had probably belonged to Eric. Although I used the chalks no attempt was made to teach me letters or numbers: that was the school's province.

My first day at school, accompanied by my mother, was achieved without fuss. I attended the Infants' department at Pendragon Road School for boys and girls. The room I was admitted to was large with a cheerful open fire, pictures on the walls and had small chairs arranged around the room in a horseshoe shape. We were given shallow rectangular tin trays with a layer of sand in them and a straw each. It was intended that we should blow into the straw to trace patterns in the sand. I was not very impressed by this as I already had a wooden box at home half-filled with sand which gave me many hours of quiet play by myself. In the midst of this non-event I could not understand why a ginger-haired girl called Vera Harris cried all the time until her mother came to fetch her for lunch.

The admission class was Class 6 and over the next two years we would proceed upwards until we reached Class 1, sometimes perhaps skipping a class. We were due to go up to the Big Girls or Big Boys' at age seven so there must have been fairly rapid progress for most. I 'went up' to Class 5, possibly 4, then to 3 from where I was desperate to move to Class 1. Almost at the crucial time I developed a cold and a high temperature and had to stay in bed for a day or two. One evening as I lay in bed feeling ill and sobbing, I knocked on the floor with the hairbrush, a signal for my mother to come up. She lit the gas and tried to make sense of my moaning "Miss my exams, miss my exams", which to me meant I would surely miss my longed-for elevation to Class 1. My mother calmed my fears with the promise that she would explain my absence and 'send a note' to the school. When I was barely recovered I returned to school with another 'note' which requested that I should not be made to sit for long in a draughty corridor while waiting to perform the little playlet in which I had been previously rehearsed. In this I was a little girl with several of my classmates, boys and girls, dressed as my toys. The content and purpose of this playlet are lost, but it was rehearsed, or performed, in the Headmistress's room. I chiefly remember the dress I wore, probably made for the school by my mother. It was pale mauve in a soft silky material with a trimming of tiny pink rosebuds around the waist.

During the winter Eric and I each had our separate interests. Eric had a model railway with Bassett-Lowke engines, coaches, line and signals. It was a red letter day for me if he set this up through the bedrooms and I was allowed to watch, perhaps even putting an engine back on the line if it fell off on a curve. He also collected postage stamps and cigarette cards and spent much time with these in his bedroom.

My indoor pastimes centred around my dolls, Mary, Topsy and Wendy and tea parties for them using the green china tea-set Grandpa Valiant had given me one Christmas. This was always carefully put away afterwards in the correct slots in the pink cardboard in the box.

My other abiding interest was my Zoo of lead animals which I gradually built up. I had an elaborate procedure for playing with them on the table. They were housed in two shoeboxes which were equipped with strips of old white flannelette sheets which, when the boxes were empty and turned upside-down, became a substitute for the snow on the Mappin Terraces for the two polar bears. A small hand-mirror made a pool, and fences clipped together made enclosures for the other animals. It was more interesting to save up to buy animals rather than fences, so my father augmented my few shop-bought fences with carefully soldered together metal ones made from wire. These had a special way of linking them together to make enclosures of different sizes. I had an elephant and a camel, both of which walked around free, several different monkeys, a hippo, a crocodile, an ostrich, deer, and two kangaroos, and maybe others. I bought them all from my tuppence a week pocket money. When the Zoo was set up I often made a list of Feeding Times for each animal in a half-size exercise book. As the animals were made of lead you could write quite well with the hippo's stumpy tail if a pencil was not to hand. When the game was finished all the fences were dismantled and put flat in their boxes and the animals carefully interleaved on top between the flannelette strips. The heaviest animals at the bottom, and so on. They were given as much care as if they had been fragile porcelain. Reading also became a hobby, and my father brought home my first library book "The Story of a Wooden Doll" from the Marylebone Public Library. I suspect it had as many pictures as words to read.

As well as my parents' 'make do and mend' policy they also took the trouble to look after what they had. An example of this would be the garden deckchairs. Neighbours propped theirs in the back garden against the fence on the asphalt summer and winter, with the result that the canvas perished and the chairs had to be replaced each year. Ours were brought in for the winter and so lasted for many years, but the only storage space, apart from a built-in cupboard in the front bedroom over the stairs, was the loft, to which my father gained access by means of a folding stepladder placed beneath the trapdoor. With head and shoulders into the opening he could then heave himself up to standing on the un-boarded ceiling joists. This was where the deckchairs were stored. Coming down was a little more hazardous and once he missed his footing and knocked over the stepladder. His shouts brought us running, to find him hanging by his fingertips to the trapdoor opening, not daring to drop down for fear of breaking an ankle on the upturned stepladder below. It was hastily re-erected, he came down and all was well again. The small push-along lawn mower also needed to be kept in a dry place over the winter and before the aviaries were built, giving room for garden tools also, it was brought indoors. It was too difficult to get it into the loft, so it spent the winter in the bathroom, between the lavatory and the bath. I can remember spelling out its name emblazoned on the handle – Velo – – – something.

In the same vein of getting the maximum use from everything, when new shoes were bought for us extra space was allowed at the toes so that a small wodge of cotton-wool could be placed there and removed as we grew. Shoe soles were also mended and one of my studio photos clearly shows a half-sole repair to my brown leather button-barred shoes. The fashion started for black patent leather shoes with an ankle-strap when the Shirley Temple films were all the rage, but as I disliked intensely the babyish, smirking film-star I was not sorry that none were bought for me. It was probably thought that the patent leather would show scratch marks, and you could not polish them with Cherry Blossom wax shoe polish! Neither was I bought the new crepe-soled leather-topped sandals when these became popular, as it was felt they caused the feet to become over-heated. Instead, we persevered with my fairly cheap rubber-soled, canvas-topped, button-bar summer shoes. These were scrubbed if necessary each evening and whitened with a kind of pipe-clay. They were left to dry overnight and for me were a part of summer, with summer dresses. But for all my parents' economies there was never a feeling of having to go without necessities, and money was found for luxuries such as our summer holidays.

CHAPTER FIVE

My mother's sewing – three and a half outings – malt and milk -
books and games – Northover shops – medical matters –
the trick – Boxhill – Eric's exam

My mother was of necessity entirely self-taught, but she
nevertheless became an excellent dressmaker and needlewoman.
She understood the value of following the proper procedure to
produce good results with her treadle Singer Sewing Machine
and always used bought tissue-paper patterns. These were
discarded when finished with but not wasted. About once a year
I would cut them into suitable-sized pieces and thread them
with a large-eyed needle on a string carrying a big button at
the end. They were then hung as toilet paper in the lavatory.

The dresses my mother made for me utilised Sale remnants
or passed-on dresses of the Aunties, and I believe I was always
well, if not expensively, dressed. She also made all her own
dresses, and after her father died she refused to wear black but
made herself a dress in an acceptable pale mauve shade. At about
that time, probably using her father's insurance money she
bought herself a china dinner service with a black and white
Art Deco design border for special occasions, as she said he had
not bought her a wedding present. Curtains were also made for
both summer and winter use, pyjamas and, of course, worn
sheets were turned 'sides to middle'. It was always an enjoyable

morning for me when I was stood on the table one April day to try on the previous summer's dresses. Some needed their hems let down, others were discarded as too small, or perhaps lengthened with toning material, and new dresses planned. My mother was also a keen knitter, and was never without a garment in progress. Knitting was an entertainment as well as a useful skill and on family social visits it was quite acceptable to take one's knitting.

My mother once took Eric and I to Peter Pan's Pool, which we always passed on the tram to Catford. The Pool was alongside the road and it was large enough to have a Wendy House on an island in the centre and a row of small boats moored and ready for hire. Behind the Pool was a Fun Fair and a children's play area with swings and slides. We had taken a picnic and were then enjoying the slides when I fell at the bottom and cut my knee on the gravel. There was much blood and dirt and in those days no handy cloakrooms to clean up accidents. Eric was sent off with a teacup and instructions to find some water. He must have been about ten and found a supply – perhaps there was a refreshment stall. I was duly cleaned up with hankies but was left with a scar for ever. I do not remember ever going there again, which was a pity.

There were two further outings which occurred at about this time. One was to the Aldershot Military Tattoo when my father was given complimentary tickets for a small party. The problem of how to get there was solved when he found a neighbour, Mr Titterton, who had a car. With my father and Mr Titterton in front and his son Peter and Eric and I squashed in the back we drove to Aldershot for the show. All went well until we found the car again at the end in the huge car park. For some reason the car refused to start and it was some time before help was found and adjustments or repairs were made and proved successful. It must have been almost midnight before we arrived home and my mother would have become anxious about our safety.

We also took a trip on the Golden Eagle, a paddle steamer, which plied from London down the Thames to Southend-on-sea. The outing was rather disappointing as after we had disembarked at the end of the mile-long pier and taken the little train along its length, we found that the tide was in and we could only sit miserably on the sloping stone sea wall and wait for the return journey with the sea lapping languidly on the muddy-looking foreshore. It was nearly dark when we started on the return journey, and we were quickly hurried past a game of Crown and Anchor spread out on the lower deck as most of the players and their supporters were noisily inebriated. It was explained to us that it was a kind of betting game.

This catalogue of not totally successful trips must end with the failed picnic with neighbours when we took our tea to a local park on a hot sunny afternoon. We had hardly arrived at our chosen spot when storm clouds piled up and we decided to dash for home. We only just got there before the heavens opened and rain lashed down, splashing up again in sheets. I insisted that we could have a perfectly good picnic if we all sat on the floor and let our current pet budgie out of his cage to fly around like a wild bird. The grownups were not at all keen, and as the budgie had once fallen into the goldfish tank, flapped his wings madly and water flew everywhere, perhaps they had a point!

In an attempt to ward off infections and keep us healthy we were given cod-liver oil and malt one day every week for a time, about a teaspoonful each. The malt disguised the fish-oily taste and we found it quite acceptable. For economy's sake my mother used to buy a large seven-pound jar of malt and decant it into a smaller jar for everyday use. I loved to watch this process. As my mother tilted the big brown jar tucked under her arm a thick tongue of the malt would appear which was expertly aimed at the neck of the smaller jar some six inches below. Although both jars were held perfectly still the tongue of malt pleated itself back and forth as it fell into the small jar and the level crept up the jar sides smoothly. I found that fascinating to watch, and there was the chance of a spoon to lick afterwards! A similar preparation was also given at school on Fridays, presumably to children whose home conditions fulfilled the conditions. We all received a small bottle of milk each day at school, and Eric told me once of being 'milk monitor' and having to collect, with another boy, a crate of milk from Verdant Lane to carry back to school. The milk had frozen and all the cardboard tops had popped up, so the crate was put near a radiator in his classroom to thaw out. As far as he knew no-one died from this lack of hygiene!

Comics were delivered with the newspaper for both of us on Saturdays. Mine was Chick's Own to start with, and Eric had the Gem or the Magnet. We would spread these on the floor and resting on our fronts read with concentration until reminded, in my case anyway, to do the weekly pocket money jobs. For my tuppence a week I had to clean the brass door knobs to all the rooms, and the brass keyhole plate on the front door, which needed a cardboard mask around it to shield the paintwork. A Council workman painted the letterbox black about once a year, leaving a matchstick propping open the flap until it was dry.

I owned very few books, but during the pre-eleven years acquired several girls' annuals and two school prizes in 1935 and

1936 for achieving "second place in test". A swimming pool and a library were built on land 'up the top', which provided access to the Dr Dolittle books and many others. The only books that I am sure Eric owned were Kipling's 'Rewards and Fairies' – a school prize, a semi-magical adventure storybook, and Grandpa's Rupert book, which I coveted but was never given or allowed access to.

As winter turned to spring we were able to play out in the street. The first game of the year was usually Whips and Tops. Eric's top was a superior pale wooden pear shape with concentric grooves around it. Mine was much rougher in brown wood, mushroom shaped with a flat top on which I chalked coloured circles. The trick was to find a chink among the paving slabs to hold the top upright, having wound the string of the whip around it several times. A quick jerk, and the top would spin away to be kept going with the whip as long as possible. There were not too many people needing to pass by on the pavement and the exercise on a brisk March day was warming. I once saw a boy bowling a hoop on the other side of the road, but it seemed rather uncontrollable and tended to roll into the road. The other favourite street game was marbles, bowling your marble to hit and claim your opponent's. I enjoyed this and sometimes took my marbles to school for playtime. I had a favourite 'winning' marble called Tommy Atkins for its prowess, and the only one I named.

Skipping, solo or in groups, in playtime at school was a good game too, with its various rhymes and chants.

"Teddybear, Teddybear, touch the ground,

Teddybear, Teddybear, turn right round,

Teddybear, Teddybear, show your foot,

Teddybear, Teddybear, sling your hook!" …ducking quickly out of the rope!

One of Eric's solitary pastimes was a kind of cricket played with two cylinders (possibly large cotton-reels) whose sides had been cut to form six surfaces. Each surface was numbered. One reel represented the batsmen and the other the number of runs scored, I believe. Eric spent some time in his bedroom rolling these along his bedroom windowsill in his imaginary games, and the rattle could easily be heard downstairs. Was this game an invention of my father's, or a copy of a game on sale at the time? It fascinated Eric and could have been called "Cricket Solitaire".

In the summer Norman and I would play 'over the fence', he on his side and I on mine. One game involved imaginary racing trains, in silhouette much like the 21st century streamlined monsters, which could drive over competitors trains while in motion! I would be the driver, inside a loop of stout wire we had found and attached by its ends to the fence, and I swayed with the (imagined) motion of the train. Norman was the intrepid guard who made 'dangerous' journeys along the outside of the train (along a foot-high narrow wall in his garden) making repairs, etc. All very exciting and our train was called 'The Silver Streak'!

If someone came in to the garden to play I could make a kind of tent on the grass, using deckchairs, folded, on their sides, with garden rakes and hoes across the top to support old curtains as covers. More like a burrow than a tent, and rather airless. We later had a three-sided garden shelter which was also useful as a tent, with old curtains covering the open front.

Eric and I both had scooters. Eric's was made by his Grandfather in wood, and painted a deep maroon colour with gold line detailing. I believe it carried his name and address, and also had a brake pedal for the back wheel. My scooter was small, made of tin with solid rubber tyres on blue painted wheels without spokes. I loved it and used it often, particularly to go 'up the top' to the shops. Other children later sported scooters with spoked wheels and white tyres, rather larger than mine, but I was happy with the one I had.

On one occasion I was sent to buy a pound of icing sugar. This was sold loose and weighed into a bag. It was not finely milled but contained many lumps, of which I ate rather too many on the way home and had to be sent back to buy another pound! Before it could be used the sugar had to be put in a stout paper bag on the pastry board and rolled with the rolling pin until all the lumps were pulverised. Cooking salt was another item which had to be prepared for use. This came in a large brick shape in blue paper. It would be placed on a clean sheet of paper and I would be given a blunt knife with which to carve it up into pieces to be put into a large jar. That was quite fun to do!

Another outdoor interest we had was kite-flying. Durham Hill boasted a large open grassy hillside where my father took us with our kites. I think mine, a simple octagonal flat kite, was probably more successful than Eric's more complicated box one, or perhaps I was more interested in learning to fly it. It certainly achieved extraordinary heights until it appeared to be a mere colourless dot in the sky and I was soon able to fly it without supervision. But I was convinced it flew so well because it had Dad's hankie as part of its tail!

There was a good selection of shops at the top of Northover, including Hammett's, a dairy type of shop selling bacon and eggs, and a chemist where we once bought a bottle of Yardley's Lavender Water, price 4/7d, for our mother's birthday. Mr Knight, the grocer, had his own stamps, small red ones, obtained on purchases, and these also went into the bag in the larder. Most years, in the Spring, Mr Knight emptied his shop window, and under a heat lamp, would have a crowd of chicks scampering about, to be watched by our fascinated eyes. They were for sale, to be raised at home, but no-one we knew kept chickens. There was a newsagent and sweetshop, Bolton's, which also sold a few small toys, and occasionally I was able to add to my stock of Zoo animals. On the other side of the road were Gorston's, the butchers, a fried fish shop, and a large branch of the South Suburban Co-operative Society, selling groceries. At one time Eric and I would be sent there with a shopping list and my doll's pram to carry the shopping home. The pram had removable seat pads in the bottom, making a good storage space, but "mind you don't catch the sugar bag on that bolt there!" We always had to quote our Co-op number, 83809, to gain the dividend for our mother.

My mother bathed and bandaged grazed knees, put Golden Eye Ointment in our eyes for styes, and gave us paregoric lozenges for coughs. If the grazes became red and septic it was time for the 'Hot Boracic Lint' treatment. For this a double piece of pink boracic lint was folded into a piece of old clean hanky and dipped into very hot water. The ends of the hanky were then twisted to wring out the surplus water, the lint was given one shake and applied to the knee, followed by a pad of cotton wool and bandaged securely. After the first shock of the heat it became comfortable and the remaining dirt in the graze was drawn out on to the lint. This treatment was usually successful in drying up the graze. There were no antiseptic liquids or ointments then for domestic use. Cottonwool was not sold in small balls but in packets, and as my mother used it in her various First Aid treatments, she prudently bought it in a large roll which was wrapped and interleaved, like a Swiss Roll, with blue paper. It would have been about a foot long and five to six inches in diameter. She would cut off a 'slice' and be able to pull off pads for grazed knees and her leg ulcers.

The District Nurse who was called in for septic fingers and leg ulcers was also called to attend when I had attacks of influenza two years running while in the Infants' School. My mother sat up with me at night when I had been put into the big bed. The bedroom fire had been lit and was used to dry my sweat-soaked pyjamas which she changed several times. There were no remedies for the 'flu, but when I had recovered sufficiently I was given a bed downstairs, once in the front room and the next year, a little later in the season, in the back room, as this was more convenient for my mother. I remember being dosed with Fenning's Fever Cure, a bitter (quinine based?) medicine, followed by a grape. As I had been assured by playground wisdom that grape pips, if swallowed, would grow inside you, I was very careful to spit them out!

After the second bout of flu Eric decided to play doctor and in play several times gave me medicine-glass 'doses' of the brown ginger beer that my mother sometimes made. These, he said sternly, had to be swallowed in one gulp. I was happy to do this and enjoyed the attention until the last dose, for which he had substituted brown malt vinegar. Ugh! This handy trick was played again sometime later when a boy called Arthur Thorpe came to play in the garden, supposedly a friend of Eric's, although he wore black or grey pin-striped long trousers which was unfamiliar school wear in our area. They played "Prisoners and Guards" and Arthur was tied to a chair on the grass. His guard, Eric, kindly fed him from time to time with mouthfuls of sponge-cake which he much enjoyed, until the last portion. As he bit into this he discovered that Eric had substituted a spring onion for the jam. We did not see Arthur again.

Around that time Eric suffered badly from a number of painful boils on his back at waist level, the District Nurse was called in and prescribed poultices of an antiphlogistic to reduce the inflammation. The ointment had to be spread on a circular piece of lint the exact size of the boil area and was then held by the points of scissors to heat over a gas flame on the cooker. When considered to be of the right temperature it was applied. This treatment my mother learnt to do as it was applied daily. Later the treatment was changed to the application of Lion Ointment which was a yellowish waxy substance in a round wooden box. Eric suffered much pain from the boils and the treatment and was forced for a time to wear braces on his shorts as a belt would have been too painful. Years and years later Eric attributed the boils to poor diet, but I think the onset of puberty was the more likely cause.

From time to time a nurse attended school with her little bowl of disinfectant into which she dipped her comb before searching the next child's head for nits or fleas. She was commonly called "Nitty Nora" by generations of schoolchildren. Her findings were not announced at school, but it seems I must have picked up these creatures once as my mother had to anoint my scalp and comb through my hair with a stinging preparation. I grizzled, of course. My mother, without any justification, blamed my current best friend's shoulder length ginger hair for infecting me. My friend was Audrey Tait and we would walk home from school together, parting eventually by the pillarbox halfway between our homes. Audrey was set to move house and told me her new address. Unfortunately she kept forgetting it herself and repeatedly had to ask me what it was: I told her as she had told me, '312 St Helier Avenue, Morden, Surrey.'

My parents decided about this time to buy a gramophone, which my father had transported from the rail station at Grove Park by one of the ubiquitous boys with a cart. The gramophone was a handsome piece of furniture on four legs, with a compartment to store the records in albums. The popular tunes of the day and classical pieces which were sampled by his Keith Prowse customers were discarded when superseded and my father was allowed to bring them home. He managed in this way, and perhaps with some purchases, to amass a large collection of popular classical and operatic music, together with some well-loved songs by artistes of the time such as Peter Dawson, and Paul Robeson. We enjoyed this collection for many, many years, and with careful selection we were also able to play musical chairs at parties.

As part of his job my father needed to be able to give his theatre ticket customers some idea of the content of the Shows – more of this later – and there were a number of regular playgoers, and travellers, whom he knew by name and chatted to. They knew he had children and saved their foreign stamps for Eric, and twice sent home a bag of things 'for the children'. One bag included some fancy crepe-paper party hats, the like of which we had never seen. Each one was made of at least two colours, with cockades, fancy brims, or tam o'shanter shapes. We kept these carefully and they were brought out and used for a number of Christmases. They must have come from a hotel or wealthy house-party. The second bag contained a complete Scottish outfit for a child – kilt, waistcoat, sporran, etc., and an eighteenth century type of boy's brocade coat and trousers, with a rather well-worn 'powdered' wig. I used both these outfits in fancy dress over the years in one way or another, and even attempted to make a new white wig with cotton wool over a pudding basin shape when the original fell to pieces.

One summer we had a change from going to the seaside when our neighbour Mr Pyefinch invited us to take our holiday at a caravan site at Boxhill in Surrey. He either owned or rented a caravan there, and there must also have been hutted accommodation because we were quite a large party. Besides we four, Auntie Flo and Kath, their daughter and also Auntie Win came with us. I believe Uncle Percy came down at the weekends. There was a swimming pool there in the open air, not used very much by swimmers, and much of my time was spent happily lying in a large car inner tube, paddling along with my hands. No one else liked to do that, perhaps I was just the right size. My mother had made a Red Indian outfit for Eric the previous Christmas and Win's photos of Boxhill show him apparently crawling through the undergrowth, stalking his enemies with his tomahawk. Perhaps he was stalking the donkey riders. Another photo shows Eric, Kath and I hiking along a grassy path with chest-high foliage on either side. This was, I believe, ragwort, crawling thickly with the brown and yellow caterpillars of the cinnabar moth. The Pyefinch children decided we would make jam on a campfire, and we were set to gather blackberries to put into a billycan on the fire. They seemed to think that it would turn into jam by itself, but unfortunately it burnt and that was the end of that good idea. It was very hot at Boxhill and there was plenty to do with donkeys to ride, swings, and the pool. Poor Auntie Flo was suffering from 'bad legs' and my mother spent much time sitting with her.

Holiday at Boxhill. Auntie Flo and Kath share the holiday

Just paddling along!

Eric, the Big Chief with his tomahawk, posing on his trusty, somnolent steed

The time came for Eric to sit for the Scholarship exam to determine each pupil's next stage in education. I had no idea what a 'Scholarship' was and this was the first intimation I had that there were things in the world that were a mystery to me but that were familiar to everyone else, which gave me a sensation of uncertainty, instability and apprehension of the unknown: feelings which were to recur. I had a vague mental picture of a Scholarship as a piece of official looking paper with grey printing on it in lines and round the edges, with a picture of a rowing boat in a prominent position printed in a faded pinkish colour. Whatever it was, Eric did not achieve it. No fuss was made at home, and in the family it was kindly attributed to the often spoken opinion that he was 'highly strung' and too nervous to do himself justice in exams. There was no choice for his next school: he was to attend the Downham Central School which had a fairly non-academic syllabus. Apart from the traditional 3R's, tuition and training would be given in bookkeeping, elementary French, woodwork and metalwork and, for some, shorthand and typing. The normal leaving age would be fifteen or sixteen.

CHAPTER SIX

Housework routines — tradesmen — Grandparents' move —
visits to the Paytons — visits to the Pooleys — fishes and birds

In 1934 when Adolf Hitler was making his demands felt in
Europe I once saw a newspaper headline which, although I
could read it, I did not understand what it meant, but it stayed
in my memory. Our newspaper after delivery was tossed on to
the banister rail at the foot of the stairs, and I can clearly see
now the large block letters crying

"RE-ARM (says) Ramsay Macdonald"

Politics was one of those topics which were not discussed
in my hearing. I do remember though my mother's extreme
annoyance, as she hated 'arguments', when my father once got
into a heated though friendly debate with Mr Batchelor, our
neighbour. I suspect Mr Batchelor was a strong Labour man,
while my father by upbringing was a Conservative.

As well as being a good needlewoman my mother was also
well-organised and thorough in other aspects of housekeeping.
As a cook she provided good, if not adventurous meals in the
style of the times. These were often planned to fit in with the
different day's housework demands. On Saturdays she would
join the group of women outside Gorstons the butchers as he
held up his various joints of meat calling out their prices with
the usual cheery comments. A quick nod from a customer

clinched the sale and the meat would be wrapped and paid for inside the shop. Sometimes, as a sign of goodwill, a penny or so would be found among the wrapping paper, under the joint.

Lil often bought beef and roasted it on Sunday with Yorkshire pudding well-risen and brown, and crisp roast potatoes. It was eaten cold at home on Monday as it was washing day. The heavy mangle was swung up ready for action and apart from coping with heavy galvanised iron baths of water for rinsing, stoking the boiler fire and lifting the wet washing from there into the sink, the washing had also to be hung on the line in the garden to dry. The hard day's work ended only after the scullery floor had been thoroughly washed.

Tuesday was the day to sweep and dust the bedrooms. The remaining beef was cut into cubes and stewed with onions, carrot and parsnips. While this was gently cooking on its own the small bedroom mats were brought downstairs and beaten and brushed in the garden. The bed sheets were then changed, top sheet to the bottom and bottom sheet removed. Then the floors were swept and this produced rolls of blanket fluff. The floors would then be mopped and perhaps the linoleum polished, although not where the mats were laid. Then all the furniture surfaces were dusted and the mats brought back upstairs and replaced. Wednesday was an in-between day, perhaps giving time for some shopping or sewing.

On Thursdays it was the turn of the living rooms and perhaps mince in some form would be on the menu. Friday was the main shopping day at Catford or Lewisham, and the meal would be taken promptly, very occasionally fried fish from the shop, to leave a long afternoon. The door-key was hung on a string behind the letterbox so that we could let ourselves in if necessary. My mother always wore her working clothes covered by a wrap-around overall (made by herself, of course,) in the mornings when housework and the dirty jobs of black-leading the grate and emptying the ashes were accomplished, and she changed into fresh top clothes for the afternoon.

Although there were few private cars on our estate during the early and mid-thirties, there were a number of tradesmen using Northover and streets around. Milk in bottles was still delivered by horse and cart, with small boys trying to hitch a ride on the back to the derisive cries of their friends to the milkman "Look be'ind yer, guvnor!". The baker from Fison's bakery had a cart which he pulled, rather like a covered-in rickshaw and he brought bread to the door in a large basket on his arm. He had large and small loaves or you could buy half a large loaf, and when my mother bought a new bread-knife she passed on her old one to the baker as the saw blade was an improvement on his straight, blunted blade. He was a little man with a nut-brown face and dark twinkling eyes like currants in a bun.

Occasionally the muffin man came on a Sunday afternoon with his tray on his head and his bell, but he did not do well and went elsewhere. In the early summer the street would ring to the cries of "Pea – oh, Pea – oh, tuppence a'pand peas" as a horse-drawn flatbed cart was driven slowly along Northover and housewives came out with their baskets and bags to buy. It was said that the cart was driven down from Lincolnshire. Shelling peas was fun, to see who could get the most peas in a pod, eleven sometimes, or even fourteen. Maggots, and there were some, were hated and carefully discarded with any bad peas. An "ice-cream man" would sometimes ride slowly along on his tricycle with a bell. Perhaps the "Stop-me-and-buy-one" Wallsy, or better, the Eldorado or, better still, a smaller firm selling "Meadow" ice-creams, rather softer and creamier. Walls's Snofrutes, frozen flavoured water ice in triangular cardboard tubes, were cheaper and very popular.

There was also the Sweetman who had his stand, a cycle with a yellow-painted little sweetshop on the front. His pitch was almost opposite our house and on as many lunchtimes as I thought I could get away with it, perhaps two or three on school days, I would beg "Can I have a ha'penny?" The answer would usually be "See if there's one in my purse." There always was, and I would buy an ounce of sweets to eat on the way back to school. Tray toffee with a thick chocolate top was my favourite and this had to be broken into small chunks to fit into the tiny bag. There was often another Sweetman further along the road on our side but he was not so popular. His "shop" was brown and he was a rather grumpy and cross little man. To encourage trade there was supposed to be a "lucky ticket" in some bags, but I never heard of any customer who found one. The dustcart, drawn by a horse, came every week. Dustbins with a great deal of coal ash in them were emptied into hoppers along the side which had lids pulled over them when full.

In 1934 Grandpa sold his cycle shop business and with Win and Ivy both doing well in secretarial jobs it was possible for the family to move. Sadly, by this time Grandpa was crippled with rheumatoid arthritis and had to use crutches to get around the house. They found a very pleasant newly-built house, number 27 Stoneleigh Park Avenue, in Shirley, near Croydon in Surrey. This was a two-bedroomed house with a dining room and sitting-room, kitchen, bathroom and separate lavatory on the ground floor, with an extra small room downstairs which was ideal for Grandpa's bedroom. New furniture, carpets and fittings were bought throughout. There was a pleasant garden

Grandma and Grandpa's new house at 27 Stoneleigh Park Avenue, Shirley

Family group in Grandma's garden

at the back with a garage, and a year or two later Win bought a car. Grandma and Dorrie shared the back bedroom decorated in blue with single beds, and Win and Ivy's colour scheme in the largest front bedroom was pale pink and pale green. Both bedrooms were equipped with wash-hand basins. The elegance of the Aunties' bedroom impressed me greatly, with their new, modern bedroom suite in light oak and new curtains and carpet bought to add further luxury. When we visited I would often go upstairs to find them finishing their toilette, and perhaps one of them would be sitting at the dressing-table buffing her nails and the other might be straightening the new pale green plump eiderdowns on the beds over toning bedspreads. It all seemed quite filmstar-ish to me. They were kind and loving towards me although not demonstrative, and between them they nicknamed me "Veramarykin". Dorrie was a Sunday School teacher, also playing the piano and sometimes arrived home late in the afternoon of our Sunday visit. Dorrie was interested in natural history and perhaps she would show me an unusual caterpillar she had found and had in a jar in the garage. I was also a caterpillar enthusiast and kept some of the furry tiger-moth kind, feeding them on appropriate leaves, once achieving a whole cycle of caterpillar, chrysalis, moths and caterpillars.

On arrival once greetings were over my father would sit with Grandpa in the dining room until the table was required for tea, and again afterwards, where they played non-stop games of cribbage. The declarations and terminology of the game were familiar to me as my father had taught me cribbage and also the soldiers' card game 'Brag'. We were always given a splendid tea with homemade cakes and, a real treat, Sunnyspread Honey. The Aunties, Grandma, my mother and Eric and I would sit on the new easy chairs in the sitting room during the evening and very moderate drinks would be consumed by the adults. They always gave Eric and I raisin wine under the impression, I believe, that it was not alcoholic, but it was and I was often asleep or ill on the last leg of the journey home by tram. We enjoyed our visits but I always found Grandpa's greetings rather a trial owing to his prickly moustache. Grandma, however, mostly made up for it by slipping a sixpence into my hand as we said goodbye. She also once gave me a chocolate Easter Egg in the form of rabbit with a pretty necklace draped around it. Win and Ivy would sometimes come to tea with us on Sundays and would bring their embroidery. They used Anchor Stranded Cotton and embroidered tray cloths, hand towels, hankies and other small items. I would watch in fascination and longed to sort and smooth the pretty silky skeins, but I was not invited to and I was too shy to ask for permission.

Four generations. Frederick Payton, Frank, Eric and Henry Valiant

My father remained close to his Aunt Nan and Uncle Fred Pooley whose son Fred married Doris, and with whom we stayed on several occasions. Fred was known in the family as "Young Fred" and he and my father had a happy bantering relationship, a little sharp on Fred's side, but his eyes twinkled and his moustache bristled as the jokes flew between them. Fred and Doris lived near Chertsey in Surrey and one of our earliest visits to them was probably the only time we spent Christmas away from home. Although it would have made a welcome change for my parents, my memory is of feeling empty and bereft at the prospect of going without our own Christmas preparations; the decorating of our small artificial Christmas Tree, and the hanging of paper chains, paper balls and bells in the two rooms. Most of our Christmas presents had to stay at home unopened until our return as we could take only one or two with us. We were no doubt made very welcome by Fred and Doris who was a short, plump, rosy-cheeked aunt with a warm smile and a calm and comfortable presence, a good foil for Fred's cheeky and sometimes abrasive personality.

Our summertime visits to them were always enjoyed and included fishing picnics by the river Thames at Chertsey. Eric and I fished with nets for tiddlers for bait for Fred, and we were admonished never to touch the reeds growing at the water's edge, as the sharp edges of the leaves "would cut your fingers to the bone!" On one such picnic, Fred baited his line and also one for my father, as Frank's first attempt at fishing. Comfortable grassy places to sit were found on the bank, Eric and I were busy with nets and jam-jars for tiddlers, and having propped the two rods almost horizontally on the bank the adults settled down to chat and await developments. Suddenly the cry went up "Frank, quick, you've got a bite!", Fred's eye had caught the subtle twitch of the float out in the river. Up jumped my father, grabbing his rod, and standing with a backward slant and heels braced against the sloping bank, he hauled on the line. Being a complete novice he knew nothing about "playing the fish" – drawing it gently shorewards, reeling it in carefully. He just heaved on the line, causing the rod to make an alarming U bend. With a mighty whoosh the fish left the water, my father fell on his back on the bank, and on the line the fish flew over our heads to land beneath a tree on the other side of the path. Great excitement everywhere and to Fred's shouts of "Don't touch it! Stand back! Don't pick it up!" we clustered around to find that Frank, the absolute beginner, had landed an 8 to 10 inch pike, a great achievement. Fred's cautions against handling it were well-founded as it was equipped with fierce spines along its dorsal fin. A never-to-be-forgotten picnic!

At Pottery Cottage
Back Row: Uncle Fred, Harry, Jack Ive, Young Fred
Middle: Leslie's wife, Aunt Nan, Grandpa Valiant,
Kit Ive (Fred and Nan's daughter), Doris
Front: Leslie's son, Alan Ive, Roy and Geoffrey Pooley

During our weekend visits we were taken to various places such as Virginia Water and Windsor Castle. After one Sunday morning local walk while Doris and my mother prepared lunch, we returned to the sound and smell of runner beans boiling on the stove. These were the first I had ever seen and were grown by Fred in his garden. We had never had such things at home and, ever cautious, I was not at all sure I would like these bits of green vegetable! Eric and I had to share a bed on these visits, which neither of us was used to, Eric, of course, having his own bedroom, and he made his resentment of this sharing plain to me. He pinched up a ridge in the bottom sheet between us down the length of the bed which I was not supposed to cross even in my sleep, and he also complained bitterly about my mop of frizzy hair annoying him on the pillow. We visited my father's Aunt Nan and Uncle Fred in their Pottery Cottage at Ottershaw nearby and on one occasion able-bodied men were set to clearing the end of the garden of weeds, nettles and brambles. Perhaps Fred and Nan had recently moved there and the garden was just too long for Uncle Fred to manage without help. So Young Fred, his brother Harry and my father spent some time hacking at the overgrown jungle to great effect. Unfortunately a toad lost its life when it became impaled on a garden fork.

Our next visit to Pottery Cottage showed a very different garden with blooming flowerbeds, including a riot of many-coloured scabious, together with trellises and arches. Uncle Fred was clearly a patient gardener and, squatting next to him I watched and learnt how to 'bud' roses. This was a technique in vogue at the time of grafting a two-inch slip of rose stem on to another rose bush, so that roses of two (or more) flowers of different colours could be produced on one bush. I subsequently saw several standard rose trees in Bromley Gardens which had been 'budded' and were sporting several different coloured blooms on each plant.

A visit to Windsor Castle with Fred and Doris

Pottery Cottage, Ottershaw

Uncle Fred and Harry were also keen model railway enthusiasts and were in the process of making a railway track round the garden. They both worked at an engineering firm in Weybridge (Short's?) and were able to machine parts of engines and rails on the lathes there. Since Harry was never called up to the Forces during the war I have wondered whether perhaps he was in a Reserved occupation as an engineer; nothing was ever said and he was a very quiet and shy man. Fred and Doris's eldest son Geoffrey was about fifteen months old when we first saw him. He seemed to me to be a very demanding and spoilt child as I watched Fred with endless patience coaxing him to eat, in his highchair, with every spoonful becoming an aeroplane before swooping towards Geoffrey's unresponsive and reluctant mouth. There is a later photo of Eric and I paddling with Geoffrey when he looks about four and he soon had a baby brother, Roy, whom I never met.

During one weekend visit we saw Young Fred's aviary in his garden, built up against the neighbouring fence. His enthusiasm for his new hobby of breeding budgerigars interested my father greatly. Now that our garden was flourishing perhaps he felt inclined to take up a new hobby, and soon began building an aviary against the house wall at the back and the neighbouring eight-foot high fence. Before it was finished we happened to be visited one Sunday by Aunties Win and Ivy. Eric and I had been instructed by our father to say nothing about the aviary to them. Perhaps he wanted them to see it only when it was fully functioning with birds in residence, but whatever his reasons he was entitled to speak about his new hobby in his own time. As I stood with Win and Ivy at the window looking out into the garden they saw that something was under construction and one asked idly "Are you going to keep chickens?". In a blind panic, mindful of my father's instructions, I could make no answer but turned and fled from the room. Apparently this was seen as the height of bad manners by my aunts, of whom I was always a little in awe, and copious explanations and apologies had to be made by my embarrassed parents.

When the aviary was finally ready my father made a special Sunday morning visit to Club Row, a market in London specialising in the sale of pets and pet supplies. No doubt he had Fred's advice in mind for his selection of birds and arrived home with a small cardboard box containing two pairs of budgerigars, blue and green. They were duly installed in the aviary, but some months later at nesting time my mother was alerted by a commotion in the aviary to find one hen bird attacking the other hen and killing its chicks. Much blood, and feathers everywhere. This unfortunate and upsetting event probably led to my father's decision to build a larger aviary at the far end of the garden where each pair could be separate in their own compartments.

When the new aviary was established my father joined the local Cage Birds Society which held its meetings in the nearby Durham Hill School. Its members bred not only budgies and canaries of all kinds but also finches. In the spring they held one or two country rambles which were most enjoyable days out. Several members would be on the look-out for nests, usually chaffinch or similar, and Eric and I became good at spotting these in the hedgerows. There would be a pause in the walk while someone reached into his inner coat or waistcoat pocket to bring out a flat tobacco tin. This was packed with cotton-wool into which one egg carefully taken from the nest would be placed, and then the tin was returned to the pocket to lie in the warmth it had come from. Placed under an already nesting hen of the same species it was a way of harmlessly increasing stock and introducing a new blood line.

The Society's Shows were held in the School Hall, and for these my father built his own show-cages painted black on the outside and white inside with perches and with soldered wire fronts to the specified dimensions. He also made a large carrying box to hold four cages for transport to and from the Shows, which were very popular and enjoyable and no doubt my father learnt a great deal from seeing so many budgies and talking to the breeders. One member, Mr Gibbs, had a chough in a large cage which collected for charity by taking proffered coins in its large curved red bill and dropping them on the floor of its cage. After several years of competing my father won a Smiths Sectric electric clock which held pride of place on the mantle-piece of our next house. The Society also organised a coach trip to Whipsnade Zoo which seemed vast to us, and where the animals were a long way away in their large fields. Auntie Win came with us and took photos of the animals to great effect.

CHAPTER SEVEN

Catford shops − trams − to the Top Class − at the dentist − Vic and
Helen's parties − the fire − wireless − theatre visits −
Patrol Leader Eric − money matters

Every week my mother travelled by tram to Rushey Green
in Catford or Lewisham High Street where she shopped for
items not available at, or cheaper than, our local shops. The shops
and stalls in both Catford and Lewisham were always particularly
busy on Friday evenings and Saturdays when pavements were
crowded with customers standing outside shops such as butchers
and fish shops which sold their wares from open displays, while
husbands and families lined the kerb waiting for them. Small
children occasionally lost their mothers but they would be
cheerfully and reassuringly hoisted aloft on to a tall man's
shoulder to see over the heads and spot their mothers. It was
always successful, no doubt with scoldings for the lost child 'for
wandering off'. On weekdays in Catford, apart from visiting
Tutts for fish, we might call at Youlls, a draper's shop. This sold
all the cottons, buttons and accessories my mother needed for
sewing, and operated one of the fascinating pulley systems for
sending cash and change to and from the cashier on overhead
lines. The grocer's shop, Sainsbury's, held much interest too for
the waiting customer and child. The skill of the assistant rapidly
catching the bacon rashers as they were sliced to the customer's

preferred thickness and fell from the bacon slicing machine was matched by the swift dexterity with which butter was patted into precise weights by the assistant's wooden patters. There was a choice between several kinds of butter; English, New Zealand, perhaps Irish and Australian too. The butter would be quickly deposited on greaseproof paper and skilfully wrapped without ever being touched by hand.

There were two large Department stores in Lewisham near the clock tower, known as the Obelisk. One, called simply "Tower House", was owned by the Co-Op and was not popular with my mother for some reason. The other, privately owned, was Chiesmans, which stood back from the road, with the little river, the Quaggy, running past in a concrete channel, parallel with the pavement. Chiesmans was a long-established firm and sold a great variety of goods, from cups and saucers to corsets, sheets and shirts, furniture and fancy goods. At Sale times in January and September, it attracted customers from a large area and bargains were to be had in all departments. My mother would always buy lengths of material to make up into dresses and nightwear, knitting wool to be kept and used as required, and perhaps shirts and underclothes for my father.

Trams ran from Grove Park Station along Downham Way and the top of Northover down to the trolley change pit just before the junction with Bromley Road. From the tram-stop at the top of Northover you could buy a "2d all-the-way" ticket between Suburban and Central London during the middle hours of the day, Monday to Friday. This was very useful if my mother wanted to go to the big Department Stores for their Sales at Peckham Rye. Passengers for a tram would stand in a group on the pavement by the tram-stop sign. Forming queues did not naturally occur until wartime. When the tram arrived and stopped, the conductor would stand on the rear platform, holding on with one hand while leaning out with the other arm raised to halt any traffic coming along behind the tram. Then passengers would surge out on to the roadway and climb aboard. A quick Ding, Ding on the bell told the driver when to proceed, and tickets were punched and issued.

The route from Grove Park to the bottom of Downham Way was classed as an outer suburban route and ran on overhead lines instead of the normal underground conduit. At the Grove Park terminus the trams reversed for the return journey, with the conductor smartly tipping the seats to face forwards again. When the tram arrived at the bottom of Downham Way (or Southover as it had become) it would stop to have its "plough" ejected downwards by a lever in the roadway and the arm connecting the tram to its overhead cable would be disengaged by the conductor hauling on a cable and running alongside to fix the arm-head under a clip on top of the tram. This was fun to watch, particularly if the conductor's feet sometimes left the ground as he swung the heavy bar. The tram then went on its way powered by the electric underground conduit. The tramway was run by the London County Council and its seats were upholstered downstairs but not upstairs where they were covered in a shiny red leatherette; a throwback perhaps to the days of open-top trams which would have got wet in bad weather. If we were returning home on a long journey, perhaps from Peckham, Eric and I would try to get the seats right at the front upstairs. These were alongside the stairs and were sideways on to the front of the tram. To alleviate the boredom at dusk or in the dark we would count the red lights we could see. As there were few cars and lorries which had red rear lights, the lights we saw would mostly have been on lit up adverts on shops along the way.

I was duly elevated in time to the top class in the Infants' School, one of whose duties included providing on Friday afternoons a team of two or three to collect all the inkwells from the desks and wash them out in the cloakroom, ready for refilling. A messy job but, of course, sought after as was any task with which one might be entrusted and so gained a little importance and a brief respite from the lessons.

In the top class, aged seven, I was rehearsed and played in the Pyramus and Thisbe playlet from A Midsummer Night's Dream – I played Pyramus. I remember the business of the chink in the wall and part of the dying speech

"Now I am dead,
Now I am fled,
My soul is in the sky
Now die, die, die, die, die!"

My "dying" was accomplished with the slim short wooden sword made by my father which I painted brown with a gory red end in watercolour paint. Apart from making these small playthings for us my father once also painstakingly 'glued' together with condensed milk a chocolate Easter Egg of Eric's which had been accidently broken. Eric often kept his Eggs almost from one year to the next, but mine were soon eaten. His taste changed to preferring marzipan eggs, or perhaps he found they were more durable.

Minor injuries could be treated at The Clinic which also had a dental department. Its reputation for kindliness was not very good, so when necessary we attended a private dentist, Mr Skinner, who removed some of my milk teeth by gas anaesthetic. Perhaps they were overcrowded. I was always terrified of these visits but had to endure them. A metal wedge on a short metal chain had to be gripped by one's back teeth, a red rubber mask was placed over the face and, apart from a dream of a strong wind blowing, the next I knew was stumbling into another room to rinse and come round to full consciousness. There was always a sixpence on the tiled shelf above the sink, which we spent on a Jaffa orange at the next-door greengrocer's.

Once I saw my mother sitting at the table at home quietly weeping with my father standing behind her with his hands on her shoulders. She had, I believe, had all her remaining teeth out to make way for complete dentures. There was a nauseating looking basin of bread and milk and sugar prepared for her on the table. I did not see her eat it.

Uncle Vic and Auntie Nell or, as she suddenly decided she wished to be called, Helen, her given name, would sometimes invite us to parties at their bungalow in Eltham. These tended to be peopled by Helen's relatives whom I scarcely knew. There was her sister Freda and also Frank and his sister Floss who lived in Catford. Floss appeared in a class photo with my mother, perhaps she was Helen's cousin. There were also two dark-haired very glamorous-seeming tall young men, perhaps more cousins, the twins, Hugh and Leonard. Helen and Vic were both tennis enthusiasts and Hugh and Leonard always seemed to be dressed in whites and holding tennis racquets. They would have looked just the part coming on stage through the French windows calling "Anyone for tennis?"

A feature of these parties were the enormous card games played with up to about twelve people crowded round the extended dining-table filling the room. Double the number of packs of cards were needed for gin rummy, Newmarket, 500, and so on. Another favourite game at that time was Monopoly which was played with vigour and excitement with rather fewer players. Uncle Vic's work as a printer allowed him to copy all the property and other cards for my parents. Having made a facsimile of the board and painted all the cards and properties in the correct colours, my father then tackled the houses and hotels needed. These were made of wood, in two sizes, and resembled, I thought, very short segments of sticks of rhubarb. They too were painted, red or green, and certainly fulfilled the need. All this seems a great deal of work, but apart from saving the cost of buying the Monopoly set, I am sure my father gained a great deal of interest and enjoyment in contriving such money-saving ploys.

My parents did not like money for its own sake, or just to put it in the bank, if they had a bank, but wanted the cash they had to work for them, and to avoid what they considered unnecessary expenditure. Apart from having money by 'for a rainy day', they used it for things they really wanted such as our holidays and occasional trips. My mother's careful housekeeping and dressmaking also helped to stretch my father's wages to their furthest.

We were once taken to the Crystal Palace Gardens at Sydenham where we were excited and enthralled by the really huge models of prehistoric animals lurking by the lakes and among the trees. I never found them at all threatening and at

Uncle Vic's bungalow eagerly sought out his encyclopedia showing pictures of prehistoric animals, the only illustrations I knew. One dark November evening in 1936 I was bustled upstairs and lifted to kneel on the windowsill in Eric's bedroom at the back of the house. Looking out of the window, I could see a fierce orange glow in the sky above the roofs of the houses at the top of Durham Hill. It was much brighter than the pale gaslamps in the street and the lights from the windows in the houses. "What is it, what is it?" I asked, and was told it was a big fire: the Crystal Palace was on fire and burning down. The reflected glow in the sky was spectacular. I could not understand how a building made of glass could burn like that and it was very sad. But, I thought, at least the dinosaurs would be safe as they stood in the lakes and under the trees.

The rambles with the Cage Birds club may have given my parents a taste for country walks because we occasionally went for our own Sunday rambles. We would walk to Grove Park Station, where I would take care not to step on the cracks between the planks of the wooden bridge to the platforms, for fear of falling through. We would take the train a few stops down the line to Knockholt Station and from there we would walk mostly by footpaths or over fields to Eynsford, where we could paddle in the river and have our picnic. There was only one drawback for me after these Sunday outings when at Sunday School the following week I was made to feel guilty for having missed the previous week and lost the star on my card. On one of our walks we picnicked on the edge of a field and my parents saw nothing wrong in allowing us to pick the low-growing raspberries in rows in the field. They were treated rather as a lucky bonus like blackberries in a hedge, and not as someone else's property. Our lunchtime tin of peaches went home with us unopened that day!

The decision was taken to buy a radio, or wireless as it was always called then. It was delivered and put on a chair, we gathered round, my father turned the knobs to the correct setting according to the instructions, but then nothing happened, no sound. Mr Batchelor our neighbour who was known to have a wireless was called in to help. He showed my father that a delicate touch was needed on the knobs to find the various stations and control the volume and all was well. We listened to Radio Luxembourg at breakfast time because it gave frequent time checks, and no doubt my parents discovered the news and other favourite programmes in the evenings. Children's Hour was always popular with us and my favourites were the Toytown series with Larry the Lamb, Dennis the Dachshund, Mr Plod the policeman and Mr Growser, and Castles of England by L duGarde Peach. These were plays illustrating history and battles and were always interesting and exciting, and some of the actors whose voices we came to recognise popped up time and again in different roles. There was always a rather simple character involved who had to have everything explained to him which was a great help in following the action.

Some years later, during a wartime invasion scare, the BBC News Announcers began their bulletins by giving their names, to prove that the Germans had not arrived and taken over the BBC. We soon learnt to recognise the various announcers' voices all speaking in the precise BBC manner. We knew Frank Phillips and Bruce Belfrage, but one we nicknamed "Ol' Barley

Dell", which was the nearest we could get to the unfamiliar name, Alvar Liddell!

Power to the wireless was provided by an accumulator. This was brick-sized and housed in a metal frame with a handle on top. It became Eric's job to take it for recharging, and when small holes began to appear in the legs of his short trousers it was realised that corrosive acid was leaking out as it brushed against him. Ever resourceful, my father made a plywood box to house the accumulator as a shield and the problem was solved.

Occasionally my parents were able to go to the theatre if my father was given complimentary tickets so that he could make recommendations knowledgably to his customers. If the tickets were for that same evening's performance my father, by previous arrangement, would telephone Mr Knight, the grocer, whose boy would bring the message of time and place to my mother usually in the afternoon. Then there was a rush! Eric was sent off to Bolton's to buy a bar of Rowntree's Motoring Chocolate, my parents' favourite choice, while my mother got ready for an evening out and left instructions about our tea. She would leave to walk to the station at about 5.30pm and I expect they had tea in a Lyon's Corner House Teashop before the show. On one occasion my mother forgot to put the chocolate in her bag, and as it was unthinkable for us that they should go without it, Eric ran almost all the way with it and caught up with her at the station in time.

On one memorable occasion I was taken to the theatre by the Aunties, probably using up extra complimentary tickets for a very popular musical show. They took me to tea at the Lyons Corner House at Charing Cross where I had cheese on toast and burnt my tongue. There was waitress service and the Aunties also ordered a selection of cakes, which for me was a great treat. We sat in the Stalls at the theatre to see the Ivor Novello show "Glamorous Nights". This was a musical, but I remember a mock-up of part of an ocean liner on the left-hand side of the stage which rocked alarmingly, with passengers on several levels crying out, or perhaps they were singing. I never did identify the flavour of the green layer in the tricolour ice cream bought for me in the interval.

The first Priest-in-charge of St Luke's church was always affectionately called Charlie Youngman by his parishioners. He was a very popular priest and was overseen by Canon Edge-Partington who was a fairly frequent visitor to the parish over the years. At first Charlie Youngman ran the Boy Scout Troop and Eric joined at about eleven. His first camp was enlivened by bumpy trips around the campsite in Charlie Youngman's car which was enjoyed as a mad adventure by all.

My family's connection with the Movement began with my father in boyhood. There is a photo of him in Boy Scout uniform taken when he was twelve years old and living with his Grandparents in 1909. The Boy Scouts held their First Rally of 11,000 boys in 1909 at the Crystal Palace; perhaps Frank's Troop attended as he lived in Dulwich, not far away. King Edward VIIth sent a message to the Scouts and concluded "…tell them that if he should call upon them later in life, the sense of patriotic responsibility and habits of discipline which they are now acquiring as boys will enable them to do their duty as men should any danger threaten the Empire." Frank was one of the extremely fortunate survivors of the following ten years to 1918 when they had indeed been called upon to serve their King and country.

Frank as a Boy Scout aged 12 in 1908. Although the jersey does not seem to be official uniform, he has the hat, stave, knapsack, belt, shoulder knot (to denote his patrol), long socks, boots and over-knee shorts. All set and looking to the future!

The virtues which King Edward applauded were, with others, enshrined in the Scout Promise and Law which was required of every new recruit, and the Girl Guides gave a similar undertaking on being enrolled as a member. Patrol Leaders were expected to make sure their recruits could recite and understand what they were about to promise –

"I promise on my honour to do my best, to do my duty to God, to serve the King, to help other people and to keep the Scout Law".

Over the next few years Eric gained badges and rose to become a dedicated and energetic Patrol Leader. It became his ambition for the Patrol to buy its own tent for camping on their own, and they set to work to raise money. Revenue came slowly until my mother suggested that she help them to make and sell orange marmalade. Under her supervision they chopped the oranges, collected and washed jars, and stirred the marmalade. When it was potted up and sealed it was taken round by the boys to their mothers and neighbours for sevenpence ha'penny a pound jar. It was not unusual at breakfast time for a lad to come to the door for more supplies to put in his cart. When the season for Seville Oranges was over they switched to making apricot jam which proved equally popular. This was made with soaked and chopped dried apricots and was easily made under my mother's willing supervision. Eric's aim was achieved and the tent was bought and proudly used at camp. Eric gained many Proficiency Badges on a variety of subjects and his enthusiasm was always keenly supported by our parents.

My father wanted to augment his salary if possible and tried his hand at betting on horses. He kept a scrupulous account of his winnings, losses, and any expenses and came to the conclusion that for a complete outsider to the sport there were no easy profits to be made and abandoned the scheme. He then turned his mind to Savings Clubs and in 1935 started one among the neighbours. Vic, as a printer, was able to provide suitable savings cards headed appropriately "The 35 Club" on which details of savings could be shown. The idea was to save small amounts weekly or monthly and the total amount could be drawn out in time for Christmas. Presumably Frank invested the money and gained some income from its interest. I believe it was a successful venture but I was too young to know much about it. I do remember though that once when Eric and I were sent across the road to collect a subscription from a neighbour he dropped a half-crown (two shillings and sixpence) in the road on our return. There was snow on the ground at the time and despite an extensive search the coin was not retrieved. Someone had a lucky find after the thaw, but my father of course had to bear the loss of the coin.

Apart from the time when she had her teeth extracted, the only other time I saw my mother in tears was when she was telling my father how she came to lose her handbag. I must have been about seven and she and I had been shopping in Catford. There were stalls along the kerb in the Broadway off Rushey Green, and when we reached the corner by the bank my mother decided to re-sort the shopping bags before returning home. She must have placed her handbag on the wide bank window-ledge, re-sorted the bags, and we moved away. We had gone only a few paces when she missed her handbag. We returned immediately to the corner, but the bag had gone. My mother enquired of the stall-owner who was only about six or seven feet from us. The woman denied all knowledge of the handbag but my mother remained suspicious of her. The loss of the contents of the bag as well as the bag itself was very upsetting. Apart from small items such as a pocket torch, she lost the only dress ring she ever had which had a small blue sapphire in the centre. Luckily my mother was still holding her purse and vowed she would never again take a handbag with her when shopping, and she never did, always holding her purse in her hand. I find myself doing the same.

CHAPTER EIGHT

*Sunday evening walks – house maintenance – Royalty – Sports
Afternoon – cinema visits – the new Brownie –
the new glasses – The Monument*

I moved from the Infants' School to the Junior Girls' when I was seven and in 1935 gained Second Place in the class. The prize for this was a book which I chose from a selection on the Headmistress's desk and was a typical mixture of stories for an eight-year-old – The Roundabout Story Book. By the following year when I again came Second in Class I had joined the Brownies and chose as my prize "Tales for Brownies" published by Basil Blackwell of Oxford for the Girl Guides Association. When Auntie Helen came one day she coloured one of the whole-page pictures with paints from my box and did it so much better than I could ever have done. But I did not know then or until shortly before she died many years later, that she was an artist. Any skills in the arts, in music or painting, for example, if practised openly would have been regarded in our working class society as 'showing off'.

During the summer months my parents liked us to go out as a family for a walk on Sunday evenings. Sometimes we went to Bromley Gardens to walk around the lake and listen to the band on its bandstand in the middle of the lake and to admire the fine flower beds. There was also a children's boating pool and we were each bought a yacht to sail. Eric's was quite large and a duckling once hitched a ride on it causing much amusement. My yacht was painted blue and was smaller but still equipped, as Eric's was, with collapsible sails and rigging. It was great fun getting them properly rigged and the sails set according to the wind, and sending them skimming across the pond. Adjustments to the sails would be made if they tended to sail in circles or hug the shore.

There was a phase when instead of Bromley Gardens we visited a few sites where new houses were being built and Eric and I would look for treasures such as pieces of putty left behind by the builders. This was probably about the time when my mother's sister Flo and Uncle Percy were buying themselves a small house in Albany Park, Bexley, and perhaps my parents were considering a similar move. Nothing further came of our excursions, however, and I believe that after much consideration my father was loath to "saddle himself with a mortgage for years and years", remembering the wage cuts he had suffered during the bad times in the 20's when money was short.

There were a number of advantages in living in a rented LCC house, not least the fact that maintenance was provided. On the outside, paintwork was refreshed, hedges trimmed and the Virginia Creeper planted to grow over the fronts of many of the houses was pruned back to about three feet below the guttering and from around the windows. Inside the house the walls and paintwork were decorated in turn every few years; walls distempered mainly with one or two rooms papered, the tenant making a choice of papers from several alternatives. Painting and wallpapering were done in separate years, probably on a five year rotation. If you owned your own house you would have had to pay workmen to do all this work as the idea of "Do it yourself" had not been thought of, and there were not the retail shops where paint and paper could be bought inexpensively.

After the coronation of King George VIth in 1937 the Royal Family made a number of trips to show themselves around the country and through London. This provided us with an exciting day out. We took the train to London and made our way to the Keith Prowse shop in Baker Street. My father had emptied the window of its travel and theatre posters and there was just room for us to stand inside. We could see over the heads of the crowd standing on the pavement and heard the cheers and applause as the open Royal Car drove slowly past. We had a good view of King George and Queen Elizabeth with the two Princesses, Elizabeth and Margaret Rose as she was always called then. The King and Queen acknowledged the cheers with a gentle wave from time to time. I do not remember the splendour or the majesty, but simply how *orange* their faces appeared. Heavy make-up, perhaps, against London's smoke and smuts?

We had a School Sports Afternoon each year at a local park which our mothers could also attend. The usual races were held, Egg and Spoon, Potato Race, Sack Race and various running races. In the High Jump, which had no pretensions as to style, the regular winner always ran straight at the rope and achieved an amazing straightforward high jump. The balancing race was the only one that I was any good at. You balanced a square board with a bun on top on your head and walked the length of the pitch, keeping the bun on the board and both on your head without touching them. I had a spectacular style of extreme concentration, with slow steps and arms held horizontally out at each side. I believe I won sometimes; perhaps my hair made a good platform for the board! After the Sports afternoon ended we could stay on in the park with our mothers who had usually brought a picnic for us.

Occasionally in our school holidays my mother would take Eric and I to the cinema. There was now a fine Gaumont Cinema in Lewisham decorated in the latest Art Deco style with a large stage and luxurious looking foyers and carpeted stairs. Eric would stipulate that the film we were to see should not be "all lovey-dovey", but I know we saw Nelson Eddy and Jeanette Macdonald in one or two of their popular musical films. The cinema would open at about 12:30 and after queuing to get in we would find seats in the wide, well-lit auditorium. My mother would produce sandwiches and we would have our lunch, listening to a concert given on the cinema organ which rose majestically through the stage. There would perhaps be performers at some time during the afternoon, and once we saw Flanagan and Allen performing their popular song "Underneath the Arches". Much later, during the war there were occasional Talent Shows on stage and I was once enthralled listening to a young airman singing "The Road to Mandalay" – very stirring and romantic. The cinema programme would contain the main film and a 'B' secondary film, plus the Newsreel, trailers for films "Coming Shortly", and perhaps a cartoon. If the main film was very popular, patrons, having queued outside for some time, would be allowed to stand at the back of the auditorium until seats became available.

More or less by force I was taken, aged nine, to join the Brownies in the Large Hall at St. Lukes. I did not really want to go and was shy as I would know no one already there. Mrs

Mayo was the Brown Owl, assisted by her daughter Grace who was a senior Guide. Once I became a Brownie I began to absorb the traditions and ethos of the Movement and apart from home, family and school, my interests were centred on the activities and friendships of both Guides and Scouts that lasted over the years.

My first evening with the Brownies, despite all my fears was magical. Mrs Mayo was steeped in Brownie lore, games and practices and I soon fitted in. Her trestle table was covered with a cloth embroidered with fairies and toadstools, and central to our traditional ceremonies was a green circular felt mat on which were sewn names and badges of former Brownies. The red Toadstool stood in the centre. Being already nine I soon passed the early tests and was enrolled, making the Promise -

"I promise to do my best to do my duty to God and the King, to help other people at all times, especially those at home, and keep the Brownie Law"

In a circle, holding hands, we skipped around singing –

"We're the Brownies. Here's our aim,

Lend a Hand, and play the game"

I went on to achieve the Golden Bar and then the highest badge, the Golden Hand, both of which were sewn proudly on my uniform. Along the way we had to learn how to clean shoes, tie up a parcel, wear our uniform correctly and tie a reef knot. It was harder to progress to learning to tie the sheet-bend and round-turn-and-two-half hitches. Semaphore was taught in two stages and needed much practice. "Milkman" and "Banana" were two favourite words using the first half of the alphabet. When a Brownie became eleven years old she was "flown up" to the Guides in a special ceremony. Gauze wings were pinned to her shoulders and with a strong Guide either side they took a little run out of the Brownie circle, and she took an assisted leap over the Toadstool into the waiting horseshoe of Guides. She then received a Wings Badge to sew on her new Guide uniform to show she had "flown up".What an excellent Brown Owl Mrs Mayo was, teaching and giving so many little girls an excellent start as future good citizens, happy and energetic.

In the winter on Sunday evenings, we four would sit around the table playing cards.We played 500, gin rummy, 31's, etc.They tried to teach me to play Whist, but as soon as I had understood a particular rule it seemed they would find another one. I soon got tired of being continually corrected and the Whist lessons ended. One Sunday evening while playing cards I was sniffling into my hankie and on enquiry replied that no, I hadn't got a cold, I was crying. I confessed that I did not want to go to school the next day "because I couldn't see the (black) board". My mother's enquiries at the school found that the nurse would be coming to the school for eye tests in the next few weeks, and until then I was moved to sit nearer the front of the class. Eventually, after several visits to the Clinic, for drops in the eyes and eye tests, glasses were prescribed.These were circular lenses in mock tortoiseshell wire frames with wire earpieces. I went to school with them expecting comments and questions, but nobody noticed. Although they were very ugly, they were acceptable at the time because there was nothing else, and I found the benefit outweighed their appearance and inconvenience. It was, however, common practice for glasses to be removed for Press or studio portraits. None of us wore our glasses in the two posed May Day photos taken by the local Press, either the Kentish Mercury or the Lewisham Borough News, and I found it difficult to assume a normal expression –

and it shows! My mother was also short-sighted, but as her father "didn't believe in" doctors and dentists she had to wait until she was sixteen and could pay for her own spectacles, which photos show were the pince-nez style with a retaining chain at one side.

My mother always made beautifully iced Christmas cakes. They might represent a snow scene with little white bought figures tobogganing down an iced-over marzipan hill, or on one occasion she bought a china "tea-cosy lady", meant to sit atop a knitted tea-cosy, and made her a crinoline-skirt cake instead, with panniers. These were partly crisscrossed with lines of icing, and on every cross was placed, with tweezers, a silver ball. She had a collection of food colours and flavourings and we set up a production line for the iced fairy cakes which she made in quantity and were always popular and a feature of Christmas teatimes. My mother would put a spoonful of icing on a cake, pass it to my father who would smooth it over with a wet knife and pass it to Eric or me, who would decorate it with "hundred and thousands", chocolate vermicelli or coloured "silver" balls. We all much enjoyed our culinary production line – and there were the spoons and basins to lick out afterwards as a bonus!

From an early age I had watched my mother making cakes and pastry and was puzzled by and envied the click, click, click sound as she rolled out pastry, while mine was silent with my little board and rolling-pin. I finally realised the noise was made by her wedding ring against the rolling-pin! I gradually absorbed the basic cookery skills, especially when my mother was confined to bed, in a downstairs room, with a painful leg ulcer. Later I learned how to use the treadle sewing machine, and taught myself to crochet from a Paton and Baldwins' book of patterns while confined to bed with a bad cold.

One summer we did not go away for a summer holiday. I believe my mother was suffering from a varicose ulcer, but there may have been other, perhaps monetary reasons. We had a few days out instead. On one day my father took Eric and I up the Monument in London which was built by Wren and commemorates the Great Fire of London. It is 200 feet high with 311 steps and gave fine views of London. When we reached the top my father would not stand with us at the railing, but stood close to the central staircase. When asked about this afterwards at home he said he had been afraid that if he stood by the railing and happened to sneeze, his false teeth might have come out and flown over the railing, never to be seen again! That is what he said at the time, but I wonder now whether he was subject to attacks of vertigo, which are as unexplainable as they are unpleasant and bewildering.

CHAPTER NINE

'Rehearsal' – Grecian dancers – pets – Cousin Kath – Safety First
– exams – Mayday celebrations – the Boat Race – penfriends –
the Scottish forecast – swimming lessons

After Charlie Youngman left St.Luke's the next priest-in-charge was Mr Ward. He was a young, lively and energetic man who, I believe, turned quite a few heads in the parish. Under his leadership, ably backed by the Assistant Scoutmaster, Dick Griffin, a concert was arranged. Apart from items by the youth organisations there were songs, monologues, etc., by members of the congregation. The show was entitled "Rehearsal", perhaps to excuse any amateur shortcomings.

The Scouts performed a sketch involving the Indian Rope Trick which was carefully planned. Eric brought home a hank of fine cord to be dyed 'old gold' so as to be invisible against the back stage curtains of that colour. My mother willingly used a saucepan and dye to achieve this. At the performance, the charmer played his pipe and the end of the rope slowly rose, apparently on it's own, to the 'sky', the invisible cord having been tied to the end of the rope and pulled up by a Scout sitting on a rafter above the stage. The charmer duly climbed up and disappeared, with his shirt floating down in his place. For some reason, a 'technical hitch', the shirt floated down somewhere else on the stage at the actual performance, but it was deemed a success and caused much laughter and applause.

The Brownies performed a playlet based on The Elves and the Shoemaker story, when the Elves do the poor Shoemaker's work for him overnight. I played the part of the Shoemaker's Wife, and in rehearsal Mr Ward showed me on the stage what I had to do. All went well on the night, my only worry being how to keep the little muslin mobcap on my head with all my hair springing up!

The Guides were ably supported by Mrs Ward who, from the side front of the stage sang in a strong sweet voice to piano accompaniment:

"My Grannie used to say to me when I was very small,
How she remembered well the day she went to her first Ball,
And in her dress, a crinoline, she sat from two til eight,
And how through all those hours she wept for fear she
might be late.
But Grandmama and Grandpapa had never really met
When Grandpapa asked Grandmama for the Second
Minuet.

The Ball, she said, was like a dream of blue and gold and red,
And Grandmama was quite the Belle, at least so Grandpa said.
And all the men were very smart in coats of every hue,
And one, the fairest of them all, was dressed palest blue.
But Grandmama and Grandpapa had never really met
When Grandpapa asked Grandmama for the Second Minuet.

The man in blue came passing by and chanced to turn his head.
He fell at once in love with her, at least so Grandma said.
And that is all about the Ball that I can tell you, dear,

For Grandmama and Grandpapa are sleeping over there.
But Grandmama and Grandpapa had never really met
When Grandpapa kissed Grandmama in the Second Minuet!"

About eight of the Guides in suitable costumes performed a stately Minuet on the stage while Mrs Ward sang. A semi-transparent gauze curtain in front of the dancers gave them a lovely dreamlike appearance. The whole concert was a great success and provided both cast and audience with much enjoyment and interest.

While in the Juniors at Pendragon School we took part, I believe, in a competition among local schools for dancers. Our Grecian Dancers' group, of which I was one, was entered and we danced on the stage at Catford Town Hall. We were in two groups and performed two dances, and I watched from the wings as the other older group danced and gracefully threw a large gold painted beach-ball between them and used a long garland of rope studded with artificial flowers. We wore brief mid-yellow 'rompers' from shoulder to thigh with white voile drapes from the shoulders which floated as we danced.

We must have won the competition because soon afterwards we had an exciting day out in London. We were required to wear a hat for this occasion, although we had no school uniform, and this was a problem as I did not possess one. The cheapest that my mother could buy for this one day's use was white chenille knitted beret, which we hoped would stay on my mop of hair.

The day began with a bus ride into London. We were given a lunch in cardboard boxes which we ate upstairs on the bus journey. Arriving at the Albert Hall we were packed into a dressing room with a lot of other children and watched as a big boy (aged about twelve) was daubed and painted all over his chest, back, and arms and legs with brown make-up and turned into a native warrior complete with an 'animal-skin' shield. Was I the only one who did not know what was going on? Our costumes this time were in pink sateen with pale grey floaty pieces from the shoulders. At this time I had the envied job of washing the teachers' teacups at the end of the afternoon, missing the last few minutes of the last lesson, and I had seen all the costumes hanging on coat-hangers from the picture rail in the Staff Room, and I think the staff had made the costumes for us. We had no footwear for this event but Mrs Gillham, our Headmistress who had accompanied us, peeked into the Hall and assured us that we had 'a lovely red carpet' to dance on. I believe the occasion was a Childrens' Pageant, perhaps to do with the Coronation, or Empire Day, and we were to be Britannia's handmaidens. She sat on a splendid raised throne in the centre of the arena. We formed four groups of six around her and performed our floaty graceful dance, taking up statue-like positions at the end which we had to hold until the finale. From all quarters of the Hall came lines of children dressed to represent the nations of the world or, possibly, the Empire. We felt rather sore in feet and knees by the end as our 'lovely red carpet' was made of rough durable sisal and it was painful to stand barefoot or kneel barelegged for any length of time. We managed somehow.

My parents had a black and white cat when I was very small

which had to be called 'Binkie', the same as Grandma's cat; apparently I thought all cats were Binkies. He appears in several photos of the garden but was not a characterful creature. He died about 1936 or 37, just about the time when Mrs Wheeler's dog had produced puppies. The mother was a large black spaniel-type dog with shiny very curly fur. When the puppies were only a few weeks old Mrs Wheeler would allow her neighbours children to 'borrow' one for an hour or so, to be cuddled and petted and perhaps put to bed in a shoebox. The puppy I borrowed had soft fluffy brown fur, a little gingery on the ears. Of course, I begged and pleaded to keep him when he was old enough, and as by then Binkie was no more, this was agreed. Rusty, as I had named him, was a delight – for a time. His fur remained fluffy and soft and he would put up with brushing and combing. My aim of taking him for walks failed, however, as he must have found the street too big and alarming, and just sat down immovably and no 'treats' could budge him.

One Friday evening in the winter I was on my own in the house as my parents were probably attending a Whist Drive in the church hall and Eric was at Scouts. I had finished whatever job I was doing at the scullery sink and thought I ought to turn off the gas light over the sink. I could just about reach it if I balanced one foot on the edge of the sink and braced the other against the wooden lid on top of the copper beside the sink, which was heating water for baths. I pulled the light off by its chain, but my foot pushed the copper lid to one side and my leg plunged into the hot water up to my thigh. In pain and very frightened I stood, with my dripping leg, on the back-doorstep shouting "Help! Help"! But of course no-one heard me so I had to help myself. In the winter I wore long brown woollen stockings, so removing the wet one, I dried my leg and covered it with Vaseline. My skin was not really scalded, but red and sore. Poor Rusty! On hearing the hullabaloo I made he hid behind the mangle as though it was somehow his fault, and had to be coaxed out!

As Rusty grew he became strong and energetic and it fell to my father to take him out on his lead. He seemed to be growing to be a woolly sheepdog. My parents knew nothing about dog training and Rusty, though lovable and even-tempered, became rather unmanageable out-of-doors. When my father found himself in danger of being pulled headlong down the steps into the street it was decided that Rusty would have to be re-homed. One day he went and I was told my father had found a family in Downham Way with four boys who wanted him, and it was thought they would be able to cope with his boisterous energy.

Some time later I was allowed to go on my own to a school-friend's house in Roundtable Road to choose a kitten from a litter there. The kittens, all of them delightful and interchangeable in looks, were put at the bottom of the stairs just inside the door. How to choose? After careful observation and thought I selected the one who had climbed the highest up the stairs, as being the most lively and adventurous. They had white necks, chests, under-parts, and legs, with grey and black tabby markings on head and back. He was put into a stout brown paper carrier bag, a skewer was thrust through the folded over top for safety, and home we went. He also was named Binkie of course!

In the mid-30's once Auntie Flo had moved to Albany Park she and my mother delighted in shopping expeditions together in the school holidays. Auntie Flo and cousin Kathleen, who was a little older than me, and my mother and I would meet at a Department Store such as Holdrons or Jones and Higgins in Peckham, or Chiesman's in Lewisham, or perhaps a store in Eltham. There Lil and Flo would spend a couple of hours browsing more than shopping, although at Sale time there were bargains to be bought. To keep us occupied Kath and I would be bought a bag of sweets each; one had chocolate toffees and the other had mint lumps. We would trail around after our mothers through the various departments of these big shops surreptitiously slipping our sweet papers into teapots, handbags, vases, gloves, etc., with much hidden giggling. Luckily we were never apprehended. At the end of the afternoon Kath might beg her mother to let me go home with them, and I would stay the night, sharing Kath's bed. The next day we would all meet up again somewhere else fairly briefly and return home.

Kath had a bike which I was allowed to try once. Kath became a Red Cross Cadet and worked away steadily gaining qualifications and experience. When she left school she worked as a shop assistant on the corsetry and underwear counter in a department store in Eltham and maintained her Red Cross hobby throughout. When she was about seventeen she began training to become a nurse, but gave up because she was unable to cope with the regular month's night duties they were expected to perform. I was fond of Kath and she had a great sense of humour, but our different lives kept us apart in our teens.

Cousin Kath in Red Cross uniform

Kath contracted TB just after the end of the war and was sent to St Alfege's Hospital in Greenwich. Fresh air was thought to be the best treatment at the time and the beds were outdoors on the balconies in all weathers – above the fumes and pollution of a main road. The patients were supposed to have complete rest, and my mother when visiting her was appalled by the strict rule against any occupation, even knitting! The thought of all that 'wasted time' was anathema to her. Kath recovered and eventually became nurse and first-aider at a zip fastener factory.

Her skill was praised by a hospital consultant after she had expertly dressed a long wound down the arm of a factory hand. The doctor enquired of the patient who had dressed his arm to be told "Oh, that was our Kathy", so he sent his compliments back to Kath via the patient for a job excellently done.

The London County Council was very aware of the dangers for schoolchildren of increasing motor traffic on the roads, and all our exercise books had Safety First Rules printed on the lower half of the red back cover. We were exhorted to "Look Right and Look Left before crossing the road", and the game "Last Across" was strictly forbidden. I never saw anyone playing this so perhaps their injunctions had good effect. Boys were warned not to hang on the back of horse-drawn carts and never to play games in the roadway.

My parents liked to play cards and attended the Whist Drives in the Church Hall, sometimes winning a prize of a glass vase or similar. There were also Bazaars and in 1937 some kind of Show with competition classes. For the cake she made my mother won First Prize, a half tea-service in cream with an orange and brown Art Deco design. The Fairy Cakes I entered in the Children's section also won a First Prize, a small box of chocolates, but as I was the only entrant I was not very thrilled by this award.

Early in 1938 my mother and I had an interview with the Headmistress regarding the date at which I would take the Scholarship exam. This was decided by one's date of birth, and the cut-off point which concerned me happened to be the day before my birthday which was the 16th March. Most of the girls who seemed to be my contemporaries were expecting to sit for the exam a year earlier than me, and my mother naturally wanted to know the reason for this. It seems that we stayed in the Top Class for two years, with about half the class leaving each year. Before the Scholarship exam there was the all-important "Prelim" to pass. I believe the whole class took this test to find out who was suitable to sit for a Scholarship. On the day of the Prelim my mother allowed me to choose the dress I would wear and I chose one that had pink wild roses on a white ground. The examination room was in a downstairs part of the boys' school and was entered via Roundtable Road. I must have passed this test and later sat for the Scholarship exam but I remember nothing at all about it. Several of my contemporaries who had sat the earlier exam had passed which meant that the school got a half-holiday in celebration. When the results of the next Scholarship exam was announced I was the only one in the class who had passed, so we got our half-holiday then too. I do not remember my parents' reaction at all; I expect they were pleased but would not have said or done anything likely to make Eric feel second best or a failure. A few days after the results were announced a new girl, Elaine Morgan, joined the class. She had already won a scholarship at her previous school which rather stole my thunder I thought. It was understood that I would go on to the nearest Grammar School which was the Joseph Prendergast School in Catford, whose girls we often saw in Rushey Green in their school uniforms, hats and white gloves and were always called by us "a lot of snobs".

The real highlight of the year for Class 1 was not the exam results but the election of the May Queen on the 1st May and the May Day celebrations in June. Each year the May Queen was elected from among those who had taken the Scholarship exam and the whole class voted.

Rehearsals for the various dance groups for the May Day event had been started in February and Miss Bolton, who normally taught arithmetic, would call out from class a specific group, e.g., gypsies, shepherdesses, Maypole dancers, Grecian dancers, or others who varied each year, so that gradually every group became trained.

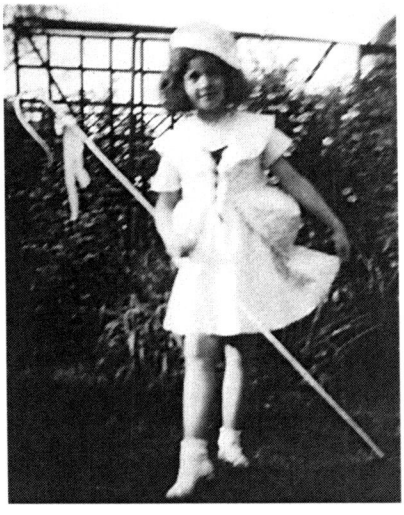

A May Day shepherdess. Costume made for school by my mother

The younger girls also participated and I was once a Blue Butterfly. There was also a Yellow Butterfly, and in costume we did our graceful little dance until struck down by "Jack Frost", a small wiry girl who could do huge leaps and springs. We were rescued by the Fairy Queen. On the May Day we performed this the Yellow Butterfly danced too near the Maypole and got her antennae caught up in the ribbons, so the Fairy Queen had to come to the rescue twice!

On the day of the festivities everyone took as many garden flowers to school as they could, and my mother usually provided me with a basketful. Outside in the playground long blue curtains would be hung over all the classroom windows to form a backdrop and chairs in tiers were arranged in rows in front of them. Two, or possibly three, thrones were positioned prominently and the school piano was wheeled outside for Mrs Gillham to play. The morning was spent by the staff in producing the plaited crowns of flowers necessary and arranging all the flowers to give the best effect. The class was supposed to be getting on with arithmetic, but once I was lucky enough to be chosen to be a 'gofer' and help the staff with the carrying to and fro of flowers, etc.

Set piece of May Queen Jean Edwards and court, posed for newspaper photo 1937

I think we must have had a half-holiday to give the staff a breather before the celebrations began, at about 5pm. Admission was by ticket and there were several rows of seats around the "arena" (the main playground), but many parents and families stood. First of all the current May Queen would process to music with her attendants in long white dresses and mount the throne. She would then be thanked, and given a little silver pendant on a chain, and I was once chosen to do this. She gave a rehearsed speech of thanks ending " – – – – and I shall always remember with pride that I was once Pendragon's (3rd, 4th, – –) May Queen". She then stepped down from her throne and was escorted to a throne at the side. If a former Queen was able to attend she would occupy the third throne. May Queens always chose the colour of the train to their dress held up by page girls, so there were delicate splashes of, perhaps, pale blue, pink, lavender or yellow. The new Queen then entered, also to stately music, preceded by a double line of six little girls from the Infants' school whose job was, in time to slow music, to sweep the Queen's pathway with their branches of may blossom. Following them, carefully walking backwards, was the flower scatterer with her basket of rose petals, strewing them in the Queen's path. The Queen was followed by six attendants in white and they took up positions on chairs by the Queen on her throne. She was duly crowned and then the dances and songs began. Each group would leave their tiered seats, perform, and return in good order to much applause. At the end all the dancers would make a huge double ring around the Maypole, and dance Sellenger's Round, a lively and energetic finish to a wonderful evening. I have always felt full of admiration for the staff of the school who worked so hard to present such a memorable evening every year. We all changed back into our normal clothes and wandered away with our mothers, very tired and still excited by the pageantry and dancing, and proud of our achievements after the months of rehearsals, until we gradually unwound at home as we had our well-earned late tea.

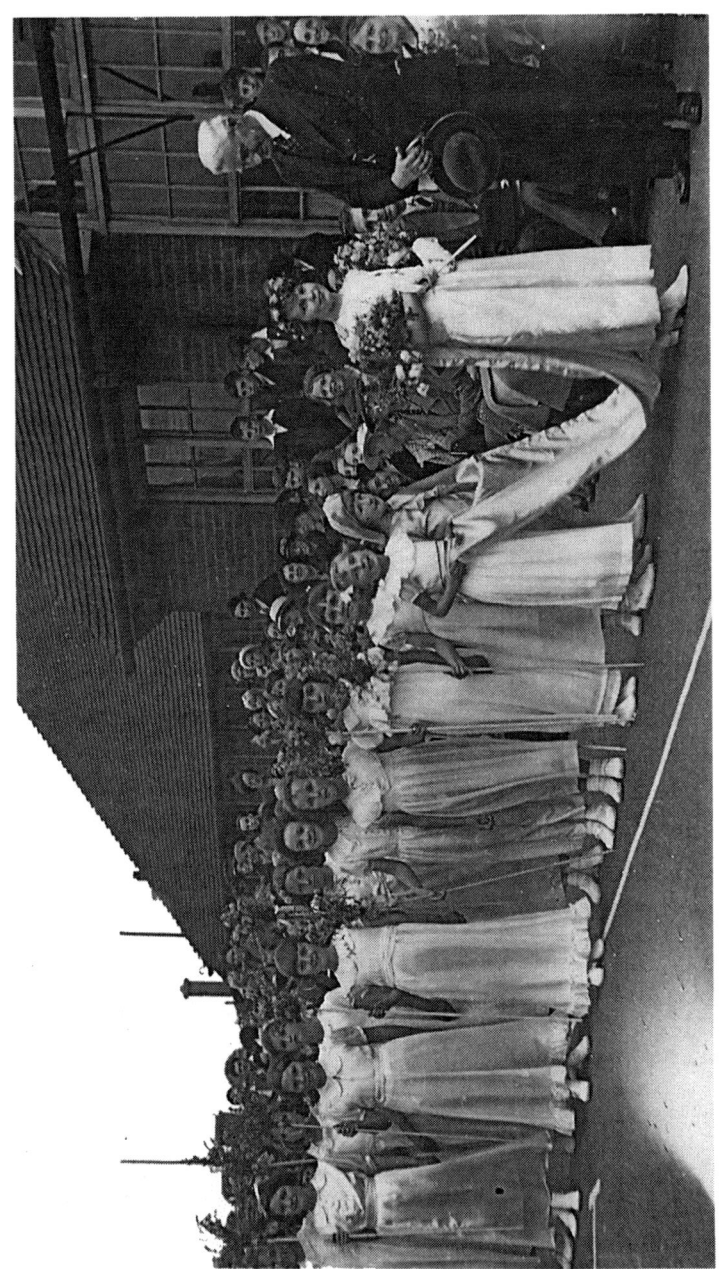

1938. May Queen Lorna Cooke with Mr. Sparkes, a School Inspector. Vera and Audrey Still in the centre.

Although there were no celebrations at school as there were for Empire Day, we children made much of the Oxford and Cambridge Boat Race. Light and dark blue favours were bought and worn proudly. Eric always supported Cambridge who were on a winning streak for a number of years so, of course, I had to support Oxford. One year in a fit of private enterprise I made a few little favours to sell at school. These were twisted up from pipe cleaners dyed pale or dark blue, with a tiny safety pin on the back. My memory tells me they were supposed to be monkeys. I charged a ha'penny each, sold a few and only one girl defaulted on payment. This was the daughter of the school caretaker, a large rough man who lived next door to the school. One year when he was in charge of taking the entrance tickets for our May Day event he put them down on a low wall beside him, and it was thought that little hands had crept through the open fence to steal the tickets and re-distribute them. Perhaps there seemed to be more people than tickets that evening! His daughter was a very unkempt and barely clean girl and the staff must have thought she was not a suitable friend for me, so my teacher 'had a few words' with me. Whatever was said, I let the association die, and I never did get the pennyha'penny she owed me!

Eric had the good fortune to spend a few days in Paris on a school trip during the Easter holidays. He came home highly excited by what he'd seen and done and seemed to talk about it non-stop for days. After that, in 1938, probably through the Scout Association's initiative, he acquired a German pen-friend. My father became increasingly anxious about the political situation in Germany and thought it best to avoid connections of any kind with Germany, and the correspondence was terminated abruptly. A previous pen-friendship had also foundered when an African boy, having requested the gift of a polo-necked pullover, sent in return a black, dried monkey skin, which soon had to be thrown away.

In Grandma's garden again. Eric is wearing possibly his first suit with long trousers!

In the Top Class we once had a visiting teacher Miss MacKenzie who was Scottish and wore a green and blue tartan skirt. She spoke a little differently from us, but it was not her accent that disturbed us, but what she said. Expecting a show of hands, she asked how many of us had had our appendix removed, and we all sat unmoving and bewildered. Then amongst other information she told us that it was expected that one in thirty present schoolchildren would die young. We all stared around us feeling apprehensive, but otherwise healthy. We were thirty in class. In fact her statistical forecast proved true a few years later. We had two unrelated girls in the class who were both called Eileen Williams, one quite ruddy-faced and wiry haired, and the other pale and quiet with big dark eyes. We learnt much later that she had died of Tuberculosis while still a child.

During our last year at Pendragon School we were taken for a few summer months to have weekly swimming lessons in the new Baths built at the top of Northover near the new library. Each must have been of short duration as we had to walk in a crocodile from Pendragon School and up to the top of Northover to the Baths and back again after the lesson. With changing and drying time, wading through the foot bath, exercises on the side of the bath and so on, our instruction and practice time in the water could not have been very long on each occasion. Although I learnt to float and swim, I did not enjoy these sessions very much as I found the echoing noises disorientating, and without my glasses and with the rubber swimming cap firmly over my ears, I could not see or hear very well whoever was calling out to me. On the way home past my house I asked permission to deposit my wet costume and towel, but this was rarely granted.

CHAPTER TEN

Brownie to Guide – new house – new school – moving house –
Nativity play – firework party – Eric's accident – the new aviary –
camp – Founder's Day.

My two years as a Brownie ended when I flew up to Guides in September 1938. I had gained several badges in various subjects, and finally the Golden Hand badge which was as far as one could go. I had begun as a new member of the Gnome Six – "Here you see the laughing Gnomes, helping mothers in their homes", we sang around the Toadstool. Then I progressed to become Sixer of the Little People – "Here we come, the Little People, we aim as high as any steeple". Now I became a very junior Guide in the Blackbird Patrol. At the approach to Christmas I was asked to wear my Brownie uniform again to represent the Pack and read a Lesson at St Luke's Carol Service. This I was happy to do as the uniform still just about fitted and I had no fears about reading aloud. The Lesson was the one from Isaiah, with the rather difficult phraseology after "Wonderful" and "Counsellor", and "Of the increase of his government there shall be no end", etc., but after rehearsing, standing in the pulpit, I managed to read it without difficulty and felt proud to have been chosen. I was just becoming familiar with the interior of the church through attending with the Guides and Brownies the monthly Church Parade for the youth organisations. The church still appeared very new and unmarked, light and airy, with light-oak coloured chairs and pulpit.

When I was about nine my parents had bought a screen for my bed to give me (and themselves) some privacy. Once I had reached the age of eleven the family was eligible for a move to a three-bedroomed house and my parents applied for one on the New Estate, as it was always called. This was under construction about half a mile away on previously green fields. We used to gather great armfuls of seedy grass for the budgies from the site where eventually the Northover Public House was built. We were given the option of two houses, at either end of a terrace of six. My mother was recovering from a leg ulcer and walked with a stick when my parents and I went to view the houses and their position, but we were not able to see inside them on that day. My father had provided himself with a compass and found that the houses faced east and west, which they thought was satisfactory. Both options had entrances with side gates in addition to the usual front door, which he had requested, for a slight rent increase. The side entrance also increased the width of the garden by several feet apart from being an added convenience.

How to choose? Near one end of the row was a site where a Community Centre was being built and my parents wondered whether the sound of noisy or musical events there might be a problem at night, with extra people coming to and fro. At the other end of the row was a fenced-off space with a green in the centre which was to become an entrance to the large field at the back of the gardens. It was planned to turn the field into a park: that sounded much better, so the choice was made –

number 66 Castillon Road, Catford, SE6. Although more than ten years had elapsed between the construction of the two estates, it was not expected that tenants would own cars and there was no provision for garages in either area, nor were the roads constructed to take public transport.

66 Castillon Road. A very low privet hedge was already planted in front. The scanty railings were removed with all the others in the road in 1940

1938 was a year when so many aspects of my life changed, and a new school, new home, and the change from Brownies to Guides meant that old ties and customs abruptly ceased. No longer the pleasant hop, skip and a jump to Pendragon School but, before the move, a walk up to the top of Northover to catch a tram to Rushey Green in Catford. By that summer I was no longer playing in the street, or with Norman over the fence, and the change from Brownies to Guides altered my social activities considerably. When we moved, my new home gave me a bedroom to myself which, though very small, was a real improvement, but my doll's cot and pram did not survive the move, nor were they really missed in all the rest of the upheaval.

I also had to have a school uniform for the first time too, the expense of which must have been of concern to my parents. After enquiries among her acquaintances, my mother had borrowed a school tunic from an older girl, Pearl Bagot, and made mine. It was very simple, navy blue, with a square neckline edged with an inch of navy velvet. Rules for the length of the slightly flared skirt were strict. For new entrants it had just to clear the floor when we were kneeling down. The older girls, such as the august Head Girl, Lilla Lamb, were allowed a longer skirt, but not more than four inches below the knee. The usual white socks, or fawn lisle stockings when we were older, white blouses and navy cardigan (both made by my mother), navy velour hat with enamel badge, and brown shoes completed the outfit. We also had to have a pair of simple, bar fastening brown house shoes and the bag to keep them in in the cloakroom. These we changed into and out of morning and afternoon. For the summer there was a choice of pink, blue, green or fawn dresses in very finely striped cotton material with white collars. Miss Franklin, our Headmistress, likened us en masse in our dresses to "a bed of hydrangeas". A navy blazer, panama hat and white gloves were always to be worn in public. A navy raincoat provided for rainy weather and the winter. My mother made me dresses in pink, blue, and green. All these new items must have represented a considerable outlay in the uncertain political and economic climate of 1939.

The Joseph Prendergast School was a Grammar School

which also had a fee-paying Kindergarten Department. It is probable that some of these pupils could, on payment of further fees, progress to the upper part of the school, but I have only one or two vague impressions of this, such as some pupils in the following year having to buy their books. Although the kindergarten girls, up to the age of eleven, had access to the playground, there were strict rules about not playing with them. I believe it was felt that some might be babied and become pets of older girls which would not be an approved relationship.

My first term at the Prendergast passed smoothly enough. It was disappointing not to be with others from Pendragon; we were all in the Lower Thirds, but they were in 'a' or 'b' and I was in Lower IIIc. Perhaps we had been streamed, or the date of the Scholarship exam determined the Form. Our classrooms were on the first floor opposite the entrance to the gallery where we sat for Prayers. The gallery overlooked the large Hall with a small stage and piano at the further end. Behind the stage rose four splendid long windows with a stained glass lady in classical drapery in each representing the school motto "Trouthe and Honour, Fredom and Courteisye", which also figured on our enamel hat badges. On one side of the hall were wall-bars for gym lessons, and on the other side were small classrooms for the kindergarten classes. They also had a large room quite apart from the hall which was also used as a dining room for those of us, including me, who took packed lunches.

In addition to obtaining a scholarship my suitability for entrance was tested by an interview with Miss Franklin the headmistress. This, it seemed to me, simply consisted of my reading a short passage to her from the other side of the room, but perhaps there was also conversation. Miss Franklin was assisted administratively by two sisters. One, known as Miss

McGregor, was tall and forbidding in a black academic gown and was probably the Bursar, and the other, known as Miss Margery must have been the school secretary, a much softer lady.

As well as the three R subjects we were used to we would have started History (I had often wondered what that was) and Geography. French was also begun by a terrifying, black-haired, sallow-complexioned French lady who insisted on speaking entirely in French. On entering the classroom she would shout "Sortez du pupitre!" while we looked at each other in consternation and bewilderment; eventually we learnt to struggle uncertainly to our feet. Her name was Miss Gare, or possibly Guerre, we did not see it written! Sometimes on Thursday afternoons we would hear tapping and hammering overhead and we were told this came from a craft lesson in leatherwork which we would be able to take the following year. Alas, that year never came.

Our Physical Exercise lessons in the Hall consisted mainly of exercises on the wall-bars and learning to climb the four or five ropes which descended from the roof nearby. Some of us managed to get as high as the gallery, but it was painful work in bare feet and legs. In later years we dragged out a box, vaulting horse and springboard and learnt to fling ourselves over these two in various ways. After one of these lessons in the VIth Form the PE teacher, Miss Burrows, insisted on inspecting our hands. *Someone* was growing her fingernails and Miss Burrows had suffered her painful grip! Always after a PE lesson we had to lie on the floor to relax for about five minutes, which ended on the command "Stand erect".

One day early in the new term I had to leave home from the house in Northover and catch the tram to Catford, but return to 66 Castillon Road by bus in the afternoon. After the move that day everything was still not straight there although my mother, with Auntie Flo to help her, had worked all day, and I was not popular when I asked when tea would be ready!

The house in Castillon Road probably occupied much the same ground area as our previous house, but the rooms were arranged differently. There was just one living room downstairs, with a three-bay window on to the small front gardens and street. At the back was a kitchen (not a scullery now) with the same un-plastered brick walls painted white, the tall dresser and high shelf along a wall. The cooking stove was electric and the wash boiler was now heated by gas, although the hand-pump for water to the bath remained the same. The bathroom was beside the kitchen opposite the front door, with a lavatory. The larder was now inside the kitchen and there was electric light throughout the house. My mother now had a small cylinder Goblin vacuum cleaner which must have been a great boon. Upstairs the front bedroom was the largest of the three, with a coal fireplace, and a gas fire was in the larger of the other two bedrooms. There was no heating in the bathroom, but we devised a potentially dangerous scheme of our own. The Valor oil heater from the kitchen was taken in and lit and placed next to the lavatory. Two towels were suspended by a large safety-pin through the lavatory chain, over the heater, and were warmed while you bathed, and the heater provided a warmish, steamy atmosphere. The fire hazard was obvious, but in those days we were brought up to use our commonsense without reliance on rules and regulations, and no towels were scorched or caught fire.

I had long been interested in words and spelling. I once spent some time at the tea table, while at Junior school, trying to work out why, on a rare packet of gingernuts, they were called 'biscuits' and spelled so strangely. I also had a phase of collecting a list of similes such as 'as white as snow', 'as black as soot', and pestered everyone for new examples. On Friday afternoons in the Top Class at Pendragon when we finished the week's work with a Spelling Test I usually scored twenty-nine out of thirty, and spelling held no fears.

Perhaps because I appeared confident with words I was asked by some of my new classmates near the end of the first term to write a Nativity Play to be performed just for the class in the Dinner Room one lunchtime. This I managed to do but nearly spoilt the result of all our rehearsing by suffering a sudden complete blankness of mind when I was to recite in the finale the verse of the carol which began "What can I give him, poor as I am?" However, I struggled through somehow, and everyone seemed pleased with our efforts.

In the autumn, with the new garden still undeveloped, we had a Guy Fawkes Night Party, and I was allowed to invite one or two new school-friends, one of whom came and was picked up later by car, an unusual event in our road. It was muddy underfoot, but we had the usual fireworks; rockets, Catherine Wheels, and handheld wavers and sparklers, a bonfire, and no doubt refreshments and everyone was happy.

Eric continued being very much involved in Scouting, being now one of the senior boys. In fact, St Luke's church and the Scouts and Guides remained the only link for us with the Downham Estate. Eric attended the usual weekend camps and either late in the autumn that year or in the early months of 1939 at a weekend camp at the site in Downe in Kent, he had an accident with a hand-axe and chopped the end of his left index finger badly. It was cleaned up and neatly bound up at the camp and put in a sling, but with a rucksack on his back he had to cycle home with the use of only one hand. After several miles it began to snow and he found he could no longer cycle. He very bravely walked, pushing the bike, for the remaining miles of the journey. My parents must have become rather worried as the evening wore on, but he finally arrived home at about ten o'clock, very tired. At the Clinic the next day he was advised to leave the dressing on his finger as it had been very well applied, and to return in a week's time. When he returned there and the dressing was removed he fainted with the pain, but it was healing well. As he was learning typing at school he was severely hampered and I remember his finger being stuck out awkwardly even when we played cards, but eventually there was no lasting damage.

During the early spring of 1939 my father worked hard at designing and laying out the garden and at Easter was able to finish making the cement 'crazy paving' paths. Kath came to stay for the weekend – perhaps Eric was at camp – and the weather was so hot we put on our knitted woolly swimming costumes as soon as we got up. We were organised into becoming labourers to transport, in several borrowed wheelbarrows, sand left over from the building of the now completed Community Centre, to mix with cement for the pathways.

A new aviary was soon built by my father at the bottom of the garden and, apart from accommodating several pairs of birds, there was room for Eric's bike and our few garden tools. Learning from his experiences, the new aviary was quite spacious for the birds with separate compartments for three or four nesting pairs, and the possibility of moving the partitions to give the young birds more room to fly about. For a time they had to be caught individually each evening and shut into the inner part of the aviary until they learnt to find their own way in. There was, of course, double netting outside to foil any cats. The field behind our garden provided ample bunches of seedy grass and other seedy weeds such as shepherd's purse. A big bundle of grass suspended in the aviary was much enjoyed with excited chirruping and bird chatter.

My father kept meticulous records and colour charts of the various breeding pairs and, as he had done previously, he sometimes sold the young budgies as pets. It was a great thing to have a 'talking' budgie and my father had hit on scheme which often worked well. He would take a young bird to work with him and rig up a perch for it across a corner of one of the customers' listening cubicles in the basement of the shop. It could fly around there for a week or two and every time he visited the bird he greeted it with the same phrase, and after some days it learnt to repeat it back to him. Sometimes the bird could later be encouraged to increase its vocabulary!

One day I saw an amazing incident in the garden – a potential disaster with a happy ending! My father was working in the aviary when a hen bird who had a nest of chicks somehow escaped. She flew high, almost describing a circle above our heads and flopped down exhausted in the garden. Binkie pounced on her immediately. My father who had run down the garden, grabbed Binkie and bundled him indoors, released the bird from him and rushed it back into its nest-box, all within minutes of its escape. The bird continued to feed its youngsters as though nothing had happened, although one might have expected it to die of shock!

The first Guide camp I attended was in the summer of 1939 at the Shaws Guide campground at Cudham, near the village of Downe in Kent. The large valley site was divided into various unfenced plots for districts in South London, each with its own equipment hut. We belonged to the Lewisham District and our hut and site was high on one side of the valley with a wood at the top. We slept in bell tents, feet to the centre, and our first task on the Friday evening was to fill our palliasse cases with straw from the pile near the entrance gate and carry or drag them over the field to the tents. On top of the palliasses we each had to have a blanket folded and pinned into a long bag shape – no down-filled sleeping bags for us in those days.

I felt very new and young and rather scared of this new experience of sleeping on the ground in a tent in a field. Without streetlights the night was very dark and we had only our small pocket torches to light us to bed. In spite of the tongue-scalding mug of cocoa we had each drunk around the fire the night felt cool and shivery. Lying in bed at last I was more than a little apprehensive to hear various rustlings and cheeps of the night creatures and birds, and I insisted on holding my comforting fifteen-year-old Patrol Leader's hand until I dropped off to sleep in this strange new environment. On the Saturday evening we all assembled in the woods and sat around the campfire. When the District Commissioner, the campfire leader, announced "There's been a terrible collision on the railway line" I really did think that was a sad item of news, but no-one else seemed concerned, and soon everyone was cheerfully singing –

There's been a terrible collision on the railway line!
The old cow didn't see the red light shine!
It happened long ago but they're working on it now –

Sorting out the engine from the poor old cow, poor old
cow, poor old cow − − −

This was a 'round' but some of the other campfire songs I found
familiar from hearing Eric singing them at home.

Towards the end of the summer term in 1939 we celebrated
the school's Founder's Day. This entailed walking about half a
mile in a long crocodile along Rushey Green, in our summer
dresses and no doubt marshalled by the Prefects, to St Mary's
Parish Church in Lewisham. The details of the service escape
me now, but I retain a strong memory of learning to sing a
setting of "Let us now praise famous men" which is now not
often sung. We needed to hold the very last note for nine beats
without a breath, and mine were not the only fingers which
beat a silent and unseen tattoo to achieve the strong and
triumphant finish. The hymn, if sung to 'our' tune, I find moving
still. So ended my first year at my new school, and the looming
threats of war and its actuality made this the only Founder's Day
I attended.

CHAPTER ELEVEN

Holiday at Cooden Beach – evacuation – New Romney –
move to Shirley Dene – to school in winter – family crisis revealed

During and after the Munich crisis in 1938 schools began to prepare evacuation plans as tension mounted in Europe. One day we had an evacuation rehearsal; at least we had to take hand luggage to school and I remember a huge pile of suitcases, rucksacks and holdalls in the classroom.

The threat of war having receded in 1939, my father had booked a summer holiday for us for the last two weeks in August, this time at Cooden Beach near Bexhill-on-sea. We did all the usual holiday activities, although Eric and I no longer built sandcastles with buckets and spades as formerly. We swam in the sea and I was able to use the laborious breast stroke I had learnt at the swimming bath during lessons while at Pendragon. I could float, but we were taught only the breast stroke which I found rather tedious and slow.

In the afternoon of Thursday 31st August we all went to the cinema and no doubt saw Newsreel pictures of the conflicts and preparations for war in Europe. When we emerged blinking into the afternoon sunlight we were confronted by placards claiming "War Imminent". This was too much for my father with the memories he had of the Great War and the prospect of fighting on British soil. He was momentarily bowled over, and had to go and sit down on a doorstep in the side road for a few minutes to recover his equilibrium, while my mother tactfully shepherded us away. It was probably decided then that we would return home the following day, Friday 1st September, instead of the Saturday.

There had been no discussion with me at home about evacuation in case of war, but it came to be accepted that I would go. All the arrangements would be made by the school and my parents had trust in the government's plans and the school's authority. The only alternative would be to stay at home with no schooling and the unknown possibilities of war. The next day, having arrived home, my father went to the school, whose two caretakers, Mr Sweetman and Mr Honey, were still on duty, fielding enquiries. He found that the evacuation had already taken place in the morning and that they had gone to New Romney, which was a little further along the Kent coast to where we could have travelled from Cooden Beach had we known. My case was packed, train times checked, and with my father I left the house on the Saturday morning for the great unknown. We were not an overly demonstrative family and we were expected to take things sensibly without fuss, and so I have no memory of an emotional farewell from my mother and Eric, although I cannot believe my mother was completely dry-eyed as she closed the front door after seeing us on our way.

At the school on Friday afternoon my father had met Mr Still, a Special Constable, who was the father of Audrey, who had been with me at Pendragon. They had arranged to meet the next day so that Audrey, her little sister Heather and I would be able to travel and be together. There was about five year's difference between Audrey and Heather's ages. Arriving eventually at New Romney Station we were directed to a hall where other late evacuees were gathered. We were handed over to the staff and our fathers left.

Now began the procedure which for most evacuees remained in their memory as a most hated and humiliating experience. We were all accustomed to the playground ritual of 'picking up' teams for games and knew that the best or most attractive children were always the first to be selected and that those remaining until the end were usually deemed the duffers and only grudgingly allotted team places. We were now confronted with number of adults, mostly women, who looked us over and would call "I'll have that one, no, not her, the other one", and so on. As the chosen ones left, with their new hostesses, those of us remaining felt unwanted and disregarded. From the reluctance of the adults now left we felt that they probably resented having to take us into their homes. Audrey, Heather and I stood together with our meagre luggage at our feet and gas masks over our shoulders, uncertain and apprehensive.

Eventually when there were very few adults left, we were assigned to an elderly lady, Miss Washington. She was accompanied by her sister, or possibly companion. It seemed unlikely that they would have had much experience in looking after children, and as the only accommodation they could offer was a little bedroom in their small house in Fairfield Road, it was possible that the facilities in the little town had been stretched to the limit, and every spare room however small had been commandeered. We were given an attic room with camp beds and mattresses which creaked dreadfully. The sash window in the room was so small you had to turn sideways to put your head out.

The following day, Sunday, 3rd September, we met with others from our school at a nearby Sports Pavilion, but there seemed to be no one else that we knew. As we sat on the benches around the room we were told at 11.15 that war had been declared. Almost immediately the Air Raid Siren sounded and we were made to crawl under the benches, and deck chairs on their sides were propped against us as a protection from possible flying glass. There could not have been more than thirty to forty of us there, so perhaps there were other venues as well for the school. There was no air raid and nothing much to do.

Our old ladies showed us with some pride it seemed, an outhouse where they had an old hand pressing machine or mangle, for sheets. This was a very large closed flat box containing, they said 'a ton of beech', or was it 'beach'? They did not explain and we did not ask. Under the box were rollers and a handle at the side to turn them. The sheets were presumably pressed between the rollers and the box to emerge flattened the other end, but there was no demonstration. I understand now that Charles Dickens described this contraption in his novel 'Our Mutual Friend' as a 'box mangle', so it was probably an antique. We went up a ladder and picked some pears for them from an espalier tree and I was stung by a wasp for the first time.

Each morning we had to report to a member of staff at a house in the town. In this way they were able to check on our welfare and, in fact, one girl had an infected toe which a teacher had to bathe and dress for her. One morning we noticed that there was straw spread thickly on the pavement and road outside the house opposite to where we met. It was explained to us that someone in the house there was very ill and the straw was to muffle the sound of footsteps or horses clattering by. We had not heard of this custom which was surely outdated, since the days of horse-drawn carriages and carts as common place traffic were long gone, but obviously the tradition had lingered on in this little town.

The weather was still sunny and hot and we might have

enjoyed time on the beach but it was nearly a mile away. New Romney had been a thriving port but in the thirteenth century a terrible storm on the Kent coast which not only destroyed the harbour at Hastings and drowned Winchelsea, but also caused enormous amounts of mud, shingle and soil to wash from Dungeness, inundating the town and swamping the harbour, which became so full of debris that the town was left almost a mile from the sea. In the hot sun, feeling lost and perhaps still apprehensive, the three of us made the journey once but finding no friends or familiar things to do there, returned to the small town. Our ladies fed us as best they could and for a suitable supper gave us milk and two or three 'hotel' biscuits each. These were plump little biscuits about an inch square, crisp and tasting of nothing; perhaps they were thought to be a treat.

After ten days during which we occasionally saw members of staff, it seemed to have been realised that there was no school for us to attend and that perhaps the Kent coast was not a good place for us to be, so near to the French coast. One morning, to the waves and cheerful farewells of the townspeople, we embarked by coach on a long drive through the sunny Kent countryside, which ended at Hildenborough, near Tonbridge. Once again Audrey, Heather and I stood about like cattle at a show, until we were allocated to the Biscoe sisters. There were three of them: Miss Edith, Miss Kate and Miss Dottie (Dorothy). They lived in a large detached house, Shirley Dene, at the end of an uphill two hundred yard drive. They kept a Cook, Gladys, a Parlourmaid, Dora Parker, and a daily Gardener, Charlie. Our bedroom was on the second floor, sharing a bathroom with Gladys and Dora. Miss Edith kindly showed us on our first evening where the pillarbox was just along the road so that we could immediately write to our parents. They must have been surprised to learn of our move, but our description of our new address would have re-assured them and in fact made them feel that we had 'fallen on our feet' with our tale of a big house and grounds, with servants, and three ladies to care for us.

In fact, we rarely saw the sisters. We had afternoon tea in the drawing room with them once, and were once taken for a walk, while they no doubt questioned us about our working class origins. We were taken to church once, probably to show us to the village as their 'war work'. The church was old, musty and dark and the service was nothing like I was used to at St Luke's. Our lives at Shirley Dene were spent either in our bedroom, in the kitchen with Gladys and Dora, or in the grounds of the house. Gladys was a round and rosy farmer's daughter who later left to train as a nurse at the local Cottage Hospital. Dora was tall and quietly dignified, but pleasant and friendly towards us and she suffered badly from head colds. We had cornflakes for breakfast except on Sundays when there was one fat pink sausage each. During term time we had lunch at school, and there would be two slices of bread and jam and a cake for our tea. Supper was either half a cup of milk, sometimes watered, or in winter, a cup of hot Oxo. We were delighted to be taken one day to the farm where Gladys had lived to pick and bring back pears which were ripe and ready for eating. We carried them back in several paper carrier bags on a pole between us. At Shirley Dene they were stored in the cellar, but we were given one each for breakfast one day. They were huge brown Calabash pears and very sweet and juicy and I wonder how many Gladys and Dora enjoyed, or whether the Biscoes had most of them, which seemed likely.

Audrey and I soon became accustomed to our new life at Shirley Dene. There was one small problem not easily solved to do with Audrey's hair. She had fair, but not blond, curly hair although not as frizzy as mine, and her mother always dressed it so that she had about five or six vertical sausage-shaped curls around her head, which can be just glimpsed in the 1938 May Day photo. It fell to me to try to copy this style for Audrey, but after various unsuccessful attempts on a number of days we had to abandon the idea. Perhaps it was time for a change of style anyway.

Soon after our arrival at Shirley Dene, the household was temporarily increased again when the Biscoes' brother Vincent came to stay for a short time. For a while a nurse was in daily attendance on him so perhaps he was convalescing with his sisters. I saw him only once; he was a big man with a loud voice who was not introduced to us, of course. At that time there was also a golden Cocker Spaniel, perhaps it was Vincent's, but it was an hysterical dog with an uncertain temper and we were not allowed near it for safety's sake. Perhaps it left when Vincent departed later in the year.

Heather was very distressed and did not settle at all well. We had to take her to the village school where, of course, she knew no one. She cried at every mealtime although we all tried our best to help her, and she returned home after several unhappy weeks.

The 29th September had been designated National Registration Day and householders had received in advance a Schedule to be filled in and official instructions regarding its completion – a list of the names of residents was required. The Schedule would be used also 'for Food Rationing purposes' and householders were advised 'It is in your interest, therefore, as well as your public duty, to fill in the return carefully, fully and accurately'. An enumerator would call to collect the Schedule and 'write and deliver an Identity Card for every person included in the return'. It was requested that he should be allowed a table to write on. We all received an Identity Card showing our name and address and our official Identity Number. My number was DJXJ 108/9 – the figure 9 showed that I was the ninth person in that household. We had to keep these cards safely, but of course as children we were never required to use them as proof of our identity. When, later in the war, the Girl Guide Association produced a small silver Guide Badge, the size of a 1p piece, on a leather strap for wearing on the wrist. I bought one and had my name and Identity Number engraved on the back, in case of need, such as injury in an Air Raid.

The other item we were supposed to take care of, and never be without, was our gas mask, in its stout cardboard box. After the box disintegrated, my mask was housed in a cream-coloured tubular metal case. We were required to take the mask to school with us every day and keep it with us wherever we went – it was a great nuisance. As there were no signs of air activity or invasion during the first nine months of the war, many adults took to leaving their masks at home, but as children we had to obey the rules. Later in the war, particularly when the country was under threat from the air or from invasion, there was strong government publicity regarding the carrying of gas masks, and Air Raid Wardens were given the task of inspecting them for serviceability from time to time.

We had a bus ride into Tonbridge every morning and quite a long walk through the town and up Pembury Rise to the Girls' Grammar School at the top of the hill. We must have put great pressure on the school's capacity and our lessons were confined to the rooms in the single-storied Annexe, which was connected but stood apart from the school. Classroom space was in very short supply and often we had to travel to a nearby village hall for lessons, or to the upper empty room in the

Library Institute in the town. Our mothers came to see us once for the day that autumn, but were not invited into the house, nor did they meet the Misses Biscoe. Mr Still came occasionally, and my father or Eric could cycle down to see us but, of course, never as often as I would have liked. Close by there was a modest roadside café, the Singing Kettle, which was useful, and also a higher class establishment, The Green Rabbit, which was really a restaurant and above our means. There was also a Post Office where we posted home our laundry if no one from home was visiting that weekend bringing us clean clothes in his rucksack on his back.

The sheets on the bed that Audrey and I shared were owned by the Biscoes and we were given old ones which unfortunately we once managed to tear, right down the middle of the bottom sheet. We laboriously sewed together the two edges, expecting to be strongly reprimanded but nothing was said; perhaps Gladys or Dora covered for us if it was they who changed our sheets.

The Biscoes owned three fields at the back of the garden of the house, which also sported a tennis court, the lines of which we were set to renew in the spring with a little push-along machine and whitening. We were not very good at keeping the lines straight. At one side of the garden was a long pond among trees with a small island at one end which was really no more than a large clump of grass with a small tree in the centre. We found a small punt there and could just manage to pole up and down and round the island which was great fun. In the desperately cold winter that year we made a slide on the pond and the depths were green and dark through the thick ice. I was never very confident on the slide as to stop you had to crash into an overhanging tree.

If from our high bedroom window in the mornings of that

winter we could see and hear men shovelling grit on to the road from flatbed lorries we knew that there had been more snow overnight and that we would have to walk to Tonbridge again to school. We had our Wellington boots, but it was about a two mile trudge through hop-fields to Tonbridge, and then to school. We tried not to be late, but it was hard going and very tiring. We were not very well prepared for such cold weather. I had hand-knitted woollen vests (numbered one to three and worn in rotation), navy fleecy knickers, white blouse and socks, school tunic and navy cardigan, raincoat and velour hat, and gloves. Exactly the same outfit would be worn until the summer. During playtime at school we had snowball fights, one side being the 'gallant Finns' – no one explained who they were or why they were gallant.

One Saturday morning at the beginning of that very cold winter, we awoke to find a deep blanket of snow transforming the trees and fields into a brilliantly white unrecognisable landscape. Immediately after our scant breakfast of cereal and tea, and stopping only to put on wellington boots and our raincoats, we rushed out into the garden and through into the fields beyond. The huge expanse of snow fascinated us as, coming from a suburban townscape, we had never experienced such an enormous snowy vista. We dashed madly about, stopping only to wonder what animals had made the occasional tracks we found near the hedgerows. After an hour or so, tired, rosy-cheeked and happy, we returned to the kitchen where we were met by Miss Edith. She was very cross with us and we were thoroughly scolded for not making the bed and tidying the bedroom before rushing out of doors. We had no idea that the Miss Biscoes interested themselves in our activities or entered our bedroom, but perhaps our small belongings and habits were investigated regularly without our knowledge when we were out of the way at school. We wore our school uniforms every day, having no occasion to do otherwise, and no other clothes with us and, apart from nightclothes, homework books and toiletries, had no other possessions. After a few months our mothers bought us knitting wool to make ourselves jumpers so that we had something to occupy us indoors. Audrey's was blue and mine was a mid-pink. But knitting in our bedroom, sitting on the edge of the bed or in an upright chair by the little table in the window was a very boring occupation and I soon grew to dislike my knitting intensely.

There was nothing we wished to buy in Tonbridge; a number of the shops had closed and it did not occur to us to buy cakes or other food to eat since school rules forbade us from eating anything in the street. Any spare pence we had bought us a few sweets from Woolworths.

Someone at school had some ice skates and we were invited to go to the local water-meadows which had frozen over to see the skating. The walk to the meadows was truly magical for me – frost and snow sparkled along the branches of the trees and glistened on the hedgerows and the pathways thick with snow. Very different too from our walks to school, a mixture of slushy paths and streets. There were not many people skating, and we had no skates, but for me the beauty of the walk and the surroundings was memorable and fantastic – a winter wonderland indeed.

Earlier during the autumn term we had been asked to choose either hockey or netball as our game to play on the sports field behind the school. My parents said it might not be worth buying a hockey stick as I might not like the game, so it was netball for me.

I did not learn until I went home for Christmas that my father had lost his job soon after war had been declared when theatres and other entertainments were closed and foreign holiday travel ceased. The little shop that he managed was closed and although the ban on theatres opening was soon lifted, the shop was not re-opened. Having survived the Depression in the late 20's and early-30's, with its wage cuts and austerity, and achieved a responsible job and a house and family, my parents must have felt not only apprehension about the coming war but also that their hard-won security was slipping away from them. Apart from the sudden loss of income my father also lost any hope or ambition he may have had for promotion, perhaps as manager of a larger shop with more responsibility and staff. He had already won a prize for window-dressing in a Keith Prowse competition, and he was by then in his early forties. I never knew of his search for work, or how many jobs he had applied for in his six-weeks search; whether he sought a position in London or tried particularly to find something in a local area. The position he finally found for which, I believe, he was eminently suited, was as an Insurance Agent for the Pearl Assurance Company whose office was in Catford. The area of his round was in Deptford and New Cross, to which he travelled by bike, but I believe it was extended during the war, possibly as agents were called up. My father had a very cheerful temperament and was able to communicate easily with all kinds of people and was meticulous in bookkeeping. No doubt this piece of family trouble had been kept from me as being upsetting, and seemed to be part of my parents' policy of not talking of family difficulties in my hearing. With no salary for six weeks during that autumn it was not surprising that they tried to keep expenses down, and I suspect that was the real reason for avoiding the sudden expense of a hockey stick for me.

When spring came at last in 1940 and we were able to punt around the pond again, we found there were sheep and lambs in the adjoining field. Peering through the sparse hedge we could watch sheep about ten feet away from us, the nearest I had ever been to any sheep. The lambs at their play were delightful. They formed a little gang of about fifteen and rushed excitedly down and up a small depression in the field, turning at the rim for a few four-footed leaps in the air, and then charging back down the little slope and up again to where their mothers stolidly fed on the spring grass. We were enchanted by their play. The island on the pond had become home to a nesting moorhen, and when disturbed by our presence, the tiny chicks fell straight out of the nest into the water, paddling away frantically after their mother to take their chance in their new watery world.

CHAPTER TWELVE

The Allotment – schooling in Tonbridge – learning Latin – the casualty – invasion scare – leaving Shirley Dene – home to school – the Co-op orders

Since we were never out after dark at Hildenborough I do not remember anything about the effects of the blackout there, but at home the nightly routine was well established. My father had made large plywood panels to fit each of the three windows in the bay of the living room which were held in place by wooden clips at the sides, and were fixed up and taken down every day. The arrangement for the kitchen window escapes me now, but no doubt it would have been equally efficient.

During the early spring of 1940, as part of the 'Dig for Victory' campaign, my father rented one of the allotments which began to cover the field behind the house. Fortunately he was able to book the plot immediately adjacent to the end of our garden and managed to fix the railings between so that we could come and go unobtrusively at will. Each plot measured 90 feet long by 30 feet wide and there were narrow pathways left between the plots. It must have taken many hours of back-breaking work to convert the plot of meadowland into friable soil suitable for sowing seeds and raising vegetables. The ground was stony clay; grass and weeds could not be pulled up by hand, they needed to be dug out. My father's life at that stage of the war was very busy and tiring, with his new job requiring constant efforts to increase the number of his clients and to collect their insurance premiums from houses and flats. After his evening meal and the necessary totalling of the money collected and the writing-up of any new policies, he would then be able to devote time to the allotment or the garden. He had also volunteered to become a part-time Air Raid Warden, and no doubt there were regular duties and patrols to perform. Since workers on a weekly wage were then usually paid on a Friday it was necessary for him to continue his round on Saturdays to be sure of being paid the weekly premiums, particularly in the case of his poorer clients.

I fear I was very ignorant and jealous of all the calls my father had on his weekends when I was homesick for a visit in Hildenborough. On the chance of a visit by Eric or my father on a Sunday, Audrey and I would walk a mile or so along the road, hoping to see a loved cyclist pedalling towards us, even if no arrangement had been made.

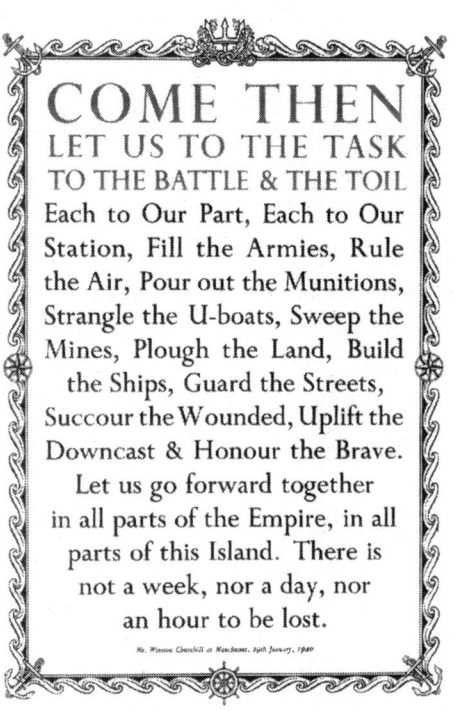

COME THEN
LET US TO THE TASK
TO THE BATTLE & THE TOIL
Each to Our Part, Each to Our
Station, Fill the Armies, Rule
the Air, Pour out the Munitions,
Strangle the U-boats, Sweep the
Mines, Plough the Land, Build
the Ships, Guard the Streets,
Succour the Wounded, Uplift the
Downcast & Honour the Brave.
Let us go forward together
in all parts of the Empire, in all
parts of this Island. There is
not a week, nor a day, nor
an hour to be lost.

Mr. Winston Churchill's speech in Manchester in January 1940, several months before he became Prime Minister

Our excursions to various halls around Tonbridge did not further our education by very much, although that did not bother us. At one village hall we were encouraged to plan a design for a long strip of woodland creatures, mushrooms, flowers, etc., to be painted on paper as a wall decoration; an ambitious idea which got no further than the teacher's momentary enthusiasm. We met sometimes at the top of the Library Institute in the town where we were supposed to do needlework, simply carrying on with hand-sewing already begun. For some reason I had no needlework to do and I was allowed to read to the class instead. It kept everyone quiet, I suppose, in the absence of a teacher, but there was no attempt to provide us with suitable reading material, one of the classics perhaps. Instead, one of the girls brought in her copies of the Girls' Crystal, a popular girls' magazine of the time, and I would sit on a desk reading the adventures of the heroines. If occasionally I came across a word whose pronunciation I was unsure about I made a quick substitution. To keep the action of the story going the character instead of saying, shouting or sobbing might have expostulated, averred, or ejaculated, which were words I was not confident about, so they were quickly altered, and no one ever noticed, and I certainly enjoyed these reading sessions.

We had to keep account of extra bus fares we might incur through excursions to other venues away from school and were occasionally reimbursed; perhaps the sum of 3s 4d would be paid to me. This I regarded as pocket money and still expected a little cash from home when Eric or my father came on a day's visit. In between their visits there would be postage to pay on parcels of laundry to be sent home. My mother, in a very rare fit of temper during my Christmas visit home, told me how much I had cost them during those first few months of evacuation while they were very short of cash. I was very shocked, of course, but as they had not previously told me that my father had lost his job and had no wages for six weeks, I could not really be blamed for not knowing money was short at home. But it made me feel guilty of somehow letting them down.

I was absent from school one day early in the NewYear which happened to be the day when the choice had to be made between learning German or Latin. I returned to school to find I had been put in the Latin group without any choice.We had lessons in the Annexe and learnt from a textbook 'Latin for Today'.The lessons invariably began with the instruction 'Discipuli pictoram spectate' – 'Pupils, look at the picture'. This always seemed to show a Roman lady in a long classical robe with a white dove perched on her hand, or perhaps it just took us a long time to get through the first lesson! We stumbled along, learning to put the verbs at the end of sentences. At some time during that term we were issued with printed cards showing family crests surmounting Latin mottoes.We were told to copy and paint the crests and mottoes – there must have been no one free or able to teach us Latin for a while. In view of my interest in words I was much later in life pleased to have had at least some grounding in Latin.

During the 'phoney war', as it was called – the months between September 1939 and the start of the blitz in the summer of 1940 – Uncle Vic continued to make frequent visits to my parents in Castillon Road, but these would shortly come to an end whenVic, Helen and their two little children, Jocelyn (Linda) andVernon, moved away.The cause may have been the closure of the printing firm which employed him, perhaps due to paper shortages, or they may have decided to evacuate the whole family together. For whatever reason, they moved to Bridgewater in Somerset, where Vic found employment with a carpet manufacturing firm. Their bungalow in Eltham was left empty, and my mother and I paid several visits to check on it before it was eventually sold. On one occasion we discovered rhubarb growing to an enormous size in a shady place and brought home sticks 'as thick as your wrist', as we could not bear to let them be wasted.

In the spring in 1940, perhaps at Easter, I was at home when Uncle Vic visited us. I was practising handstands in the garden with him helping by catching my feet, when perhaps continuing too long and being tired, I fell heavily on my back. My right shoulder hurt for the rest of the evening and I sniffled, and it was impossible for me to get out of bed on my own next morning. My mother took me to the Casualty Department at Lewisham Hospital where chaos seemed to reign. I was poked and prodded and a fractured right collarbone was eventually diagnosed. A nurse tried to find a padded splint to fit across my shoulder blades but they were all too long. All they could do was to give me a collar-and-cuff bandage sling, tell me to keep my arm inside my clothes and to return in a month's time. My mother mentioned that I was temporarily at home from being evacuated, whereupon the doctor bellowed "If I had my way all these children with broken limbs would go back out of London!" I was thoroughly upset by this time and could not see how I could manage at Hildenborough, so there were tears. It was obvious that one-armed I would need help which would not be forthcoming at school or at Shirley Dene so I stayed at home for the month. There was little I could do, no knitting or embroidery, and I tried without success to write left-handed. All I could do to fill my time was to read, and I used the Library that had been built 'up the top' near the swimming baths. I also changed my mother's books there. She had a small fat red notebook with the authors entered alphabetically and the titles she had read noted on the pages, so choosing books for her was easy. One day while I was struggling to push the books into my bag after checking them out the young assistant made some jokey remark which I did not hear, so I made no reply. To my surprise he followed me into the foyer with a red face, full of apologies as he had not noticed that I really *was* disabled with only one arm. Poor lad, he looked only about sixteen and was covered in confusion. I am sure he thought I was a brave air raid survivor, which embarrassed me too, so I left quickly before we made the misunderstandings any worse!

One Friday late in May Audrey and I left our cases packed in our room ready for a quick dash after school to catch the Green Line coach to Sevenoaks where we changed and caught a bus to Bromley and Grove Park from where we would walk home. Unusually the whole of our school was summoned to the Hall at the end of lessons and we were all forbidden to go home that weekend. Prefects had even been stationed at the school gates to prevent any girls who might have tried to sneak out and miss the emergency assembly. I am not aware that we were given any reason, it was just an order, from the local police probably. Disappointed we returned to Shirley Dene and unpacked our cases. We had even picked some bluebells for our mothers. It seems that invasion was fully expected that weekend and traffic was to be kept off the roads. Perhaps our parents would have guessed when we did not arrive home, but I knew nothing of the invasion scare at the time.

At the end of May the evacuation of troops from Dunkirk

was begun. With a friend I sat on the grass at school looking out over the town from our high position on the hill. We could see trains steaming into Tonbridge Station where some would pause. We understood that some of the school staff together with some Sixth Form girls were at the station to help with the distribution of tea and food to the exhausted troops. It was rumoured that not all the soldiers were British, and that some of them were wearing fezzes! I think we imagined that we could see the soldiers waving from the train windows too.

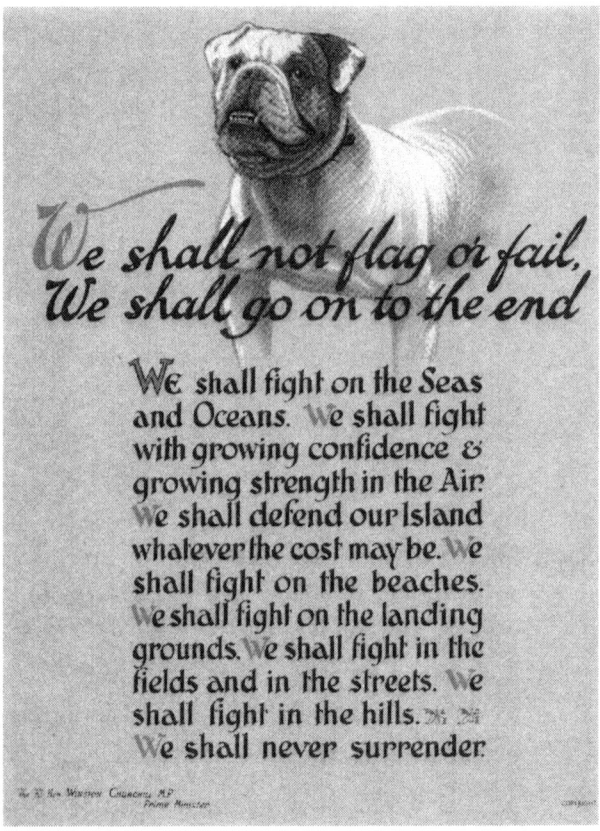

We shall not flag or fail,
We shall go on to the end

WE shall fight on the Seas
and Oceans. We shall fight
with growing confidence &
growing strength in the Air.
We shall defend our Island
whatever the cost may be. We
shall fight on the beaches.
We shall fight on the landing
grounds. We shall fight in the
fields and in the streets. We
shall fight in the hills.
We shall never surrender.

Winston's speech after the fall of France

146

Later in June, when the invasion scare had receded and I was able to go home for a weekend again, my father told me that the Prendergast School was going to re-open in Catford in September. Would I like to come home for good when the summer holidays started? Of course, I said yes – only provided I would be able to go to school! What a little prig! That was settled and I returned to Hildenborough for the last few weeks.

While I had been at home with my fractured collarbone Audrey had continued to live on her own at Shirley Dene, and Gladys, the cook, had kindly taken her home to her farm once or twice for a treat. Gladys soon left to train to be a nurse and another cook, Margaret, arrived. She was small and wiry, very different from Gladys, but endeared herself to us by baking extra French pancakes just for Audrey and I on her first evening with us. That was an unexpected and delicious treat indeed! Very, very occasionally, if we happened to be there when the remains of afternoon tea on a tiered cake plate was brought back into the kitchen from the drawing room, we might be allowed to finish up the buttered fingers of toast, cold and congealed by then, of course. I think we were probably always hungry and would have eaten anything. Margaret did not stay long and her place was taken by Dora's sister Ivy who did not have her sister's pleasant and calm nature unfortunately, considering us a nuisance in the kitchen and making more washing-up. We were not expected to help with this. The china that we all used bore the Indian Tree design, but had obviously been relegated to the kitchen because some of the pieces had been broken and were riveted together. After the end of term we paid one more visit to Shirley Dene to find the Biscoe sisters were intending to manage without any staff, and the kitchen looked very bare and empty without a cook, or even

Charlie the gardener in the corner with his cup of tea. Dora had left too, having once written in my autograph book "Remembrance is all I ask, but if remembrance proves a task – forget". I have not forgotten you, Dora.

When the Prendergast School re-opened in September 1940 it became the gathering point for any grammar school girls in the area whose schools were still evacuated. Girls from several different schools – Mary Datchelor, Sydenham Hill, Haberdasher's Askes and so on, all with different uniforms and hats arrived for the new term. During the succeeding months rules about school uniform had to be eased: the obligatory white gloves were forgotten and changing into house shoes every morning could not be enforced.

One day we were told we were to have a new girl in the class who was German. No further details about her were given, and we were asked to welcome her. As I had noticed at Pendragon, a new girl soon acquired a dazzled group of followers and Cordula Krause soon attracted her group. She was a tall, strong girl with coarse sun-bleached corn-coloured hair to her shoulders and improbable-looking black eyebrows. She spoke English well, but said nothing about her former life. She did mention once, to her appalled but delighted fans that she and her parents used to bathe naked together in the sea! Giggles and sniggers all round!

When the school re-assembled, the Kindergarten Department had disappeared and the large room became a modest Common Room as well as a Dining Room for the cold lunchers. There was a piano there and once or twice a mistress would have a group around her while she played songs for us to sing. We had used the Clarendon Song Book in our first year and had learnt a number of folk songs and sea shanties, and we now also learnt others, including a Russian folk song, and we crowded around, peering at the words over her shoulder.

Some of my mother's shopping was done at Catford or Lewisham although on moving to Castillon Road she took weekly deliveries from the South Suburban Co-op from early November 1938. Her order book bears receipts and these were given when she paid for the goods a few days after their delivery. It is interesting to trace the pattern of purchases through 1939 into 1940 when rationing of some foods, for example sugar, began. In 1939 her weekly sugar order varied between four to six pounds a week, to eight or even twelve pounds in June and July, the jam-making season. From October 1939 there are occasional stamped requests in the order book for the return of the brown paper from each parcel. In October too demerara sugar is 'unobtainable' and 'pieces' sugar (soft brown) is likewise not sent. In November the request is 'Please send your Ration Card as soon as possible', but not until the 19th December does my mother note that she has 'registered for sugar'. From 11th January 1940 she orders '3 persons sugar, gran' (granulated). The ration was twelve ounces per person per week and for three people (I was away from home then) the cost was tenpence farthing. The Ration Books would have been duly marked when she paid the bill. The order for the 6th March includes as a separate item 'nine pounds of gran for marmalade' and 'Permit – – – –' is pencilled alongside. At the end of the month, 'Butter

Ration is now 8 ounces', but my mother continues to buy her butter at Sainsbury's although the Co-op supplies her with 'Fresh Roll' which is margarine, and 'Cooking Fat' or lard. On 16th May when paying the bill she is able to buy four pounds of sugar in addition, no doubt allowed by permit in the jam-making season. From 7th December 1939 to April 1940 my mother often writes at the bottom of the order the instruction to the delivery man who called on Thursdays 'If out leave in front window'. How wonderful to be able to leave a sash window unlocked and unattended! The last order in the book is dated 18th July 1940 and is for sugar, flour, rice, a tin of (golden) syrup, margarine, white cheese and cooking fat; this item has 'regret' written by it and was not sent. The bill is for three shillings and tenpence farthing. Presumably deliveries were no longer possible to customer number 83809.

CHAPTER THIRTEEN

Life in the Blitz – at school – Lily – St Luke's on fire –
Eric called-up – breakfast routine – food rationing

The decision to re-open the school had been taken well before the air raids began and the dogfights overhead between Spitfires, Hurricanes and German aircraft heralded on 10th August what came to be known as 'The Blitz'. How quickly we became used to the sight of aircraft flying overhead! It did not seem to be many years ago when the noise of an aeroplane made us rush out and look up to see whether it was one of the new 'monoplanes' in the early 30s, or just the double-winged variety, perhaps trailing an advertising banner for Persil, Bovril or similar. Very, very rarely we might see an autogiro, as the first helicopters were named.

Anderson air raid shelters had been issued free of charge to those on a modest income from early in 1939, for householders to erect in their gardens. Ours was positioned at the end of the garden parallel with, and facing the aviary. With the excavated earth and railway sleepers and planks my father constructed a large box filled with earth about four feet tall, opposite the entrance to the shelter, as protection from blast, leaving just enough room to climb in and out. A sleeper on each side of the shelter helped to shore up the earth piled over it, which needed to be five inches deep on the top.

I did not see the installation of our Anderson shelter which took place while I was away at Hildenborough but I watched my father and other neighbours help our next-door neighbour, Mr Sullivan, a diminutive Irishman, to begin to erect his. A straight-sided hole 7½ feet long by 6 feet wide had to be dug to the depth of about 3 to 4 feet. When this had been achieved the sections of corrugated iron sheets could be installed with their curved ends meeting to form the top of the shelter. There was room for only one person at a time to excavate the hole and Mr Sullivan did his best to fill the buckets that were passed down to him and heave them up on to the side. Unfortunately water began to seep into the hole and Mr. Sullivan became increasingly unable to lift his feet from the mud which was by now several inches deep. Finally he had to give up as he was totally unable to move a step. Neighbours' strong hands under his armpits brought him cleanly up and out of the pit – leaving his boots still upright and firmly embedded in the mud! Everyone cheered and laughed at his rescue and the problem of salvaging his boots was then tackled before they filled with water. Work on the shelter could not proceed until better weather conditions caused the water to drain away again.

It must have been about this time when my mother carefully wrapped all the pieces of her fine hand-painted china tea-set and stored them in a stout wooden box, which was placed deep in the cupboard under the stairs. My father had enrolled as a part-time Air Raid Warden and Eric, at seventeen, was also a volunteer warden. I continued to go to school throughout the daytime raids, when we spent the time fairly uselessly sitting in a large ground-floor room whose outside wall had been reinforced with sandbags, or on each side of the corridor outside the room. No attempt was made to give us lessons, but we did have Spelling Bees in a casual fashion. On my return home in the afternoons I rather over-dramatised to myself the relief on seeing my home still standing at the end of the road.

Eric in uniform as a part-time Air Raid Warden

In the evenings we got into the habit of retiring to the shelter at about 7pm when the sirens usually began to wail, aircraft droned overhead and guns might be heard in the distance. One October evening before the nightly raids had established that routine I had retired to bed in the shelter some time in advance of my parents. They were most surprised to find me opening the kitchen door half-an-hour later, white-faced and shaky. "What's the matter? What's happened?" they queried.

Rather shame-faced I muttered "Spiders". I could cope without difficulty with the earwigs and woodlice from the garden intent on sharing the shelter with us, trundling across the flagstone at the entrance, and we kept an empty matchbox for their despatch tucked into the corrugated wall by the door opening for that purpose. But the large menacing spiders that in the autumn always seemed to seek indoor accommodation began to fill me with abhorrence. They moved too fast to be caught and would run over one's face, or we thought they did, when we were asleep. That night I had become particularly distressed on my own at being unable to find and swat the brute I had seen, and had stumbled through the dark garden back to the safety of the house. My dear mother calmed and comforted me and accompanied me back to the shelter, where we searched all the bedding by candle and torchlight. We did not succeed in finding the beast, but I became convinced finally that it had escaped, and was tucked up for the night, which we hoped would be peaceful. Arachnaphobia was a strange legacy from the Blitz which even now, though under some control, continues to bother me.

As I have mentioned, my father's new job as an Insurance Agent entailed much bookwork in the evenings. He also had to count and reconcile his daily takings, on policies whose premiums were sometimes for as little as a ha'penny, a penny, or tuppence a week. To help some of his cash-strapped clients in the poorer areas of Deptford and New Cross, he would encourage them to put on a high shelf an old teapot or jug, to use as a 'piggybank', and to put their pennies when they could, in that, so that when he called, perhaps fortnightly or monthly they would have the premiums already in hand. The idea of saving in this way was novel to some, and it worked. My father also needed to check the entries and perhaps write up new policies every evening in his rather unwieldy collecting book with its glossy black covers. It measured about eight inches top to bottom and ten inches wide. This would be opened out flat to twenty inches and was held along his left arm when calling on clients. The names and addresses were on the left and the columns for payment on the right. Copying out all the names, addresses and policies into a new book each year was a major task in which we helped in checking the entries. In the confines of the shelter there was no room for a table but, ever resourceful, he rigged up an electric doorbell from the shelter to the kitchen so that he could work there, when not on Warden's duty, and my mother could summon him to the shelter if she thought the air raid was coming too close for comfort. My mother and I would knit and read by candlelight in the shelter, and I also embroidered an apron for my mother with garden flowers, probably from an iron-on transfer from a magazine. We were very fortunate that there was no bomb damage very near to us during the Blitz, but we saw it all around us and buses were often held up or re-routed according to road disruptions.

One evening when my father had made our nightly cups of cocoa, he made his way down the garden and carefully put down the tray near the shelter opening and turned round to enter the shelter backwards. The noise of approaching aircraft suddenly became much louder and, with only one foot down into the shelter, he was grabbed and heaved backwards – he and Eric collapsing in a tangle of legs and arms. We were all laughing too much to hear any further aircraft droning overhead, but at least the cocoa was not spilt!

One winter evening when Eric and I had gone down to sleep on our mattresses on the floor of the shelter, we remarked how cold our feet seemed to be. Investigation showed that several inches of water had seeped into the shelter and soaked the mattresses. For the rest of that night my mother made me a bed on the floor in our living room up against a central house wall. In the morning, late for school, I made sure to take a note explaining what had happened and that after the disruption we had been very late in finally getting to bed. Of course, we were not alone in finding water in the shelter; the underlying clay soil in the area made the problem widespread, and workmen soon came from the Council to add two more inches to the cement lining, up to nearly two feet tall at the sides, making a small shelf all round. Condensation was a problem, and although there was a narrow ventilation tube poking out of the top of the shelter, we still hung bags of salt inside which had to be regularly dried off for further use.

Newspaper photo headed 'The Fire Raid in London' – St. Paul's Cathedral on Sunday 12th December 1940. The caption read 'Splendid, Serene, the Shining Symbol towers above the fires of Hate'.

The education I received at school during the next phase of the war was no doubt the best that could be managed with the staffing difficulties they faced, but it was necessarily of a much lower standard than would have been maintained in peacetime. In 1941 and 1942 there was no sense of preparing for the School Certificate examinations we would face in 1943. The staff teaching science seemed to change constantly, with little enthusiasm, and inexperience showing through. We had two History mistresses, Miss West and Miss Willoughby, both of whom were university graduates, one of Oxford and the other of Cambridge. Although there seemed to be a little rivalry they were the best of friends, and it was rumoured to our puzzlement that one had gained her MA after examination, but the other simply paid a fee for hers – true or false, we neither knew nor cared.

The only member of staff who appeared to work hard to teach us was Miss Mobbs, or Mile-a-minute-Minnie, as we called her. When we took our places in the classroom she would already be there, writing on the blackboard with incredible speed for what she called 'ten minutes mental'. She would cover one, if not two blackboards with mental arithmetic questions which we had to answer in the first ten minutes, to speed up our thinking capabilities. We ploughed on through geometry and algebra, but when we started on logarithms, tangents, cosines and such I could feel I was losing my grip. We were still learning Latin, with Miss Forbes, who wore open leather sandals which we felt showed a Roman influence. Miss Franklin, the Headmistress, had retired at the end of the last term at Tonbridge, shaking hands with every pupil and wishing us all well in her gentle way. Our Headmistress now was Miss Odell of whom I retain minimal impressions. The two Misses MacGregor vanished at the outbreak of war. There was nothing my parents could do to improve my education if they had even thought it necessary. It seems that advances in education, science teaching, technology and the arts throughout the 20th century and beyond have occurred so steadily that each generation of parents feels ill-equipped to keep up with their children's schoolwork, particularly in a non-academic family, which mine certainly was.

As I had no school-friends nearby to be with in early 1941 and there were no children of my age among the neighbours, I spent most of my spare time at weekends reading. During the evening we listened to the wireless while we knitted, sometimes reading at the same time. My mother thought I should be doing something more constructive in my spare time when homework was done and there were no house or garden jobs for me to do. She made enquiries and found that the Guide Company was flourishing at St Luke's, meeting on a Saturday, and I was made to go along although I was not keen, having seen none of the Guides since the summer of 1939. To my surprise I was remembered and welcomed and soon made friends. They were already rehearsing for a playlet about King Arthur and his Knights, so I became an extra Knight in a knee-length tabard in royal blue, and black woollen stockings.

My best friend became Lily Johnson who was already at work in an office of W H Smith's in London. She lived at 66 Roundtable Road. Her home life seemed a bit chaotic and her mother had just had another baby to add to the family. Lily had a boyfriend, one of the Scouts, George Osmond (Ozzie). I never really saw any show of affection between them and I think Lily really just liked the idea of having a boyfriend.

My best friend Lily Johnson

Guide meetings moved to Friday evenings after the Blitz ended and Lily and I would see a string of the younger girls home afterwards. Lily always needed to buy her rail ticket (perhaps a weekly season ticket), and George, wheeling his bike would catch up with us somewhere on our route and walk Lily home. About this time we rehearsed and put on a small Guide play, 'Joan of Arc'. As the Small Hall at St Luke's had no stage we used the hall at the Community Centre near my home. I played Joan and one or two of the other Guides in the cast were also from the New Estate, as it was still called.

After the friendship between Lily and George had foundered and we were about fifteen or sixteen Lily became quite distraught, feeling she was 'on the shelf', as the term was.

She became friendly with a work colleague, Eric Schmidt (who always preferred to call her Lilian), and dropped out of things for a while. When I next saw her, very briefly, it was rumoured that she was pregnant and had been turned out of home. She went to live with the Schmidts and married, and about three years later I visited her and her little daughter Gillian Anne in Palmers Green.

From 1941, through re-joining Guides my social life became very full. I attended church on Sundays and followed an evening weekly course to qualify as a Southwark Diocesan Sunday School Teacher. I was also persuaded to attend Confirmation Classes, run by the Reverend Derrick Underwood, then our popular Priest-in-charge, and was confirmed by the Bishop of Southwark in February 1942. Auntie Win, my godmother, presented me with a bible to mark the occasion.

Once I had become a Patrol Leader it was my responsibility to make sure that new recruits understood the words of the Promise they were about to make at their enrolment. It was similar to the Scout Promise –

"I promise on my honour to do my best, to do my duty to God, to serve the King, to help other people at all times and keep the Guide law"

On one occasion I had to calm an apprehensive recruit who imagined she would have to go to Buckingham Palace to serve the King his tea and 'did not know how she would manage'! We found this short rhyme useful in memorising the ten Laws and their order –

'Trusty, Loyal, Helpful, Friendly, Courteous, Kind, Obedient, Smiling, Thrifty, Pure in body and mind'.

One needed to be sure that an eleven year old knew the meaning of 'honour', 'loyalty', 'courtesy' and 'thrift', and the kindness to animals and obedience to grownups that was also required. The saving grace in this litany of virtues was that one promised ' ... to do my best to keep the Law'. It seems to me now that the first nine are all positive attributes to strive to attain, but that the 10th Law – 'A Scout/Guide is pure in thought, word and deed' implies refraining from thoughts, words, and deeds that might be common practice for others. Perhaps it was Baden-Powell's attempt to prevent the passing on of 'smutty stories behind the bike sheds', or the sharing of 'dirty pictures', and the general sniggering about girls/boys that has occurred between youngsters through the ages as they began to learn, however imperfectly, about life as an adult. But the problem was that if these dubious sources are to be shunned, how else would a child learn about sex, which would seem to be a shameful subject?

Our parents, in the 30's in the working classes anyway, had probably themselves learned piecemeal from innuendoes and patchy experiences, and felt that sex was not a subject that they wished, or were able, to discuss with their children. The subject might be touched on if there were new babies in the family, but in our circle of friends and neighbours this did not seem to happen. Our families had arrived in the estate with already two or three children, suitable to the size of the available houses and there was no room for extended families or grandparents. My mother, whose own mother had died when Lily was eleven, gave me only the very barest information about menstruation, following it up with the fact when you were married "if it stopped then you knew you were going to have a baby", which may have been what her mother told her. How you got to that stage was not explained.

On the positive side it meant that for me and my friends and the Scouts there was an openness of behaviour. We were really more like brothers and sisters, although I would not have put it like that at the time. We were just friends together; there was no sneaking off as couples, or suggestive remarks and giggles. Some of the Scouts and younger Guides I knew then have remained lifelong friends, which I find both amazing and enormously fulfilling. There is the point of view that we were somehow stunted in our growth and were under-prepared for adult life in this respect, but I cannot comment impartially on that view. There was also at that time the beginning of the idea that sex education was being given at school and I think some parents hoped for that solution.

At the Prendergast School we had one lesson when the PE teacher, Miss Ford, a South African, enlisted one of her acolytes to stand in front of the class bare-breasted, and I think she would have tried to talk to us about the changes in our bodies in puberty, but the class was inattentive and inclined to smirks, giggles and blushes, and she did not get very far. No further attempts were made in this branch of our education.

Although we were not aware of the significance at the time, a massive incendiary bomb raid ended the Blitz in May 1941. Even though we lived several miles away from the centre of London we received our share of these fire bombs. My father and Eric were on duty as Air Raid Wardens, and together with other householders tackled the bombs as they fell with sandbags or stirrup pumps. We were amused to see a young neighbour of ours, aged about fourteen, with a sandbag over his shoulder running about desperately trying to get to an incendiary bomb to smother it *on his own* with his sandbag! Almost opposite our house was a small block of flats of three storeys. An incendiary bomb had lodged beside a roof window and Eric crawled halfway out of the window on to the roof in an attempt to reach it where it flared. Unknown to him a stirrup pump was being organised on the roadway below, and he and the bomb were suddenly deluged by a stream of water. Comparing notes afterwards it seemed likely that my father had been in charge of the stirrup pump. Oh dear!

We heard of no property damage on our estate but St Luke's church, probably without organised fire-watchers, had been set alight; the roof of the nave was burnt and in ruins. Burning debris from the roof ignited the chairs and wooden floor below and the body of the church became gutted and unusable. The church had been built only about 15 years previously and the destruction was sad to see. The Lady Chapel alongside however was undamaged and, boarded off, became the church and just about adequate for the congregation. The Holy Eucharist was celebrated and I also often attended Evensong during which we prayed for 'our most gracious Sovereign Lord, King George, our gracious Queen Elisabeth, Mary the Queen Mother, the Princess Elisabeth and all the Royal Family'. Another prayer and response at Mattins seemed particularly apt when the war was not going well for us "Give peace in our time, O Lord, because there is none other that fighteth for us, but only thou, O God".

From the beginning of the war the call-up of young men brought changes everywhere, not least to the Scout Troop. The Scoutmaster (Skipper) Fred Parkes, whose tight authority Eric had found irksome and constricting in his mid-teens, was called-up and spent his service life in the army, mainly in Burma. The young Assistant Scouters soon left too, and the Troop was run by senior Patrol Leaders such as Eric and his friend George (Todd) Ware. Eric volunteered for the Royal Navy and was called up on 1st September 1941. He wanted to buy me a gift before he left and I chose a book (of course), 'Charles and Mary Lamb's Tales from Shakespeare' which he inscribed –

"With Best wishes to Vera
from Eric
On joining the Royal Navy
1st September 1941"

The illustrations are by Arthur Rackham and some are dated 1899 or 1909. Delightful!

Todd joined the Royal Air Force. Eric's first posting was to HMS Lossiemouth in Scotland. He was soon sent to the USA on a course for a month. I met him on his return at a London rail station just before Christmas, and found that Todd was also there having been alerted by Eric to help with his luggage, which would include his hammock, kitbag and attache case of 'rabbits', the Navy term for souvenirs. Todd was in uniform, darkly good-looking, but as shy and inarticulate as ever. We waited for Eric's train to arrive, but not exactly together! Much later Todd, as a navigator, lost his life in a bombing raid over Duisberg in Germany, a sad loss which our little community felt deeply. We all knew his mother and his sister Jane, who was in the Land Army. Among Eric's 'rabbits' were for me, a Girl Scout badge and two pairs of real silk stockings, which I thought were wonderful and so warm! We were so pleased to have Eric home for Christmas, and listening to the King's Speech on Christmas Day, I sat with toes curling and fists clenched, *willing* the king to get through his speech without too many hesitations. I suppose having a stammerer close to us we felt particularly sympathetic.

Eric in 1942

Eric was sent on a further course of training to South Africa, and later described helping on a farm and enjoying beautiful peaches. He eventually emerged from training as qualified in using underwater sonic listening devices, known as ASDIC, to track enemy submarines. He served on a frigate in the Atlantic before being sent out to HMS Anderson, the Naval Base in Colombo, Ceylon (Sri Lanka). From there he served in ships in the Pacific Ocean and on one occasion he volunteered, as one of seven, to help drop supplies over Burma to the retreating Army which was suffering badly from near starvation and lack of equipment. While in the air they were in danger of Japanese anti-aircraft fire, and watched as the dirty and ragged soldiers dashed from the trees to gather up the life-saving goods. Many years later his narrative of this event was included in a radio programme entitled 'All in a day's work', ex-servicemen's tales of extraordinary experiences.

In writing these memoirs I have become conscious that my brother does not figure very large in the account of my young life. He does not seem to have been a close presence, perhaps because of the age difference between us and I have only a few isolated incidents to relate, such as when, at about ten, he arranged a Treasure Hunt for me around the house …"Hanging behind the lavatory door you'll find a key all covered in gore …" etc. There was the time he was told to take me for a walk when I was recovering from flu. Another time he persuaded me to rush home with him after one of our Sunday family walks, so that we could 'steal' things for his Chemistry Set. As I remember, he took a spoonful of washing powder, Rinso or Oxydol. He did not help me to read or learn 'tables'. I wonder what he did during the time I played with Norman over the fence or made tents in the garden? My father had no interest in watching or playing football or cricket and Eric showed no interest in either of these, or in any other sport. What did my parents and Eric talk about? Did they discuss family matters with him, and the progress of the war? He went from Pendragon School to the Central School which was about a mile away, I believe, but I never saw it. I heard nothing about what he learnt at school; he brought home no articles of wood or metalwork and I was not aware that he helped my father to build the aviaries. Once he became enthusiastic about Scouts – he was never a Wolf Cub – he quickly became immersed in their activities, and by the time I was taking the Scholarship exam he would have been a Patrol Leader and keen on taking badges and camping.

Eric left school at sixteen and joined a firm of Chartered Accountants, always referred to as 'Lord Fosters', I suppose as a junior clerk. As I have related he became afflicted with a stammer as a young boy which became worse in times of excitement, but which was generally accepted as just part of Eric. Whether he was mocked at school I could not say, but no jeers or name-calling occurred in my hearing through the years. He tended to be slim and of a good height, but not tall, with light brown hair with the slightest touch of auburn. He had blue eyes which would open wide to profess innocence of any misdemeanour, and as a young adult and through the rest of his life had a charm of manner which endeared him to his many friends and colleagues. I think we discovered one another as friends briefly during the Blitz when we retired together to the shelter and for an hour or so talked on our own before our parents came down. When he joined the Navy I would write him long letters about school and the evening activities that filled my life then. At some time after he had started work he took a short after-work course at St Bartholomew's Hospital aimed at controlling or alleviating his stammer. He was advised to relax on his bed for half an hour each day on returning home from work, which he did for a time, but I did not learn whether this or any other treatment aided his condition.

I have no memory of how we managed for privacy when there were four of us at home all needing to wash at the kitchen sink as there was no washbasin in the bathroom. But after Eric was called up a routine emerged for the three of us which lasted until I left home. I would get up first, put the electric kettle on and in winter, light the Valor oil stove, topping up the paraffin if necessary, and place a large tin kettle of water on the top. Then I would make tea and take my mother a cup, my father not wanting any. Then I would wash at the kitchen sink. While I dressed my parents would get up and my father would wash while my mother laid out the breakfast things. We had only cereal and toast for breakfast, but because my father liked more toast than we could spare butter and marmalade for, his first slice was spread with the good fish-paste made by Tutt's the fishmonger in Catford. Binkie also had a slice of bread and fish-paste, cut into little squares on his homemade special little wooden board, followed by fish from the cods' heads we bought for him. I would sometimes take a waterproof bag to school and buy "twopennorth of cods' heads" on my way home. One large cod's head once cooked provided enough fish for several days for him, even with two meals a day. There were very few kitchen scraps or leftovers for him but occasionally we could get 'lights', animal lungs, for him.

Food rationing had crept up on us and since we had no access to extra rationed food my mother had to practice economy and much ingenuity in catering for us. Had we lived in the country we might have had access to extra eggs, butter, milk, cheese, perhaps a little meat or chicken, together with orchard and wayside fruits. During 1941 the weekly ration of meat varied from 1s 6d each in January, down to 1s 2d, then to 1s in March, to be raised again to 1s 2d in June. Obviously cheaper cuts of meat could be made to go further and slow cooked casseroles and stews with vegetables were popular, as were meat puddings and pies using suet or cooking fat if available. The sugar ration was fairly stable at 8oz, with extra jam-making allowances in the summer. Butter and other fats were around 6 to 8oz per week. Cheese was rationed to 1oz in January, rising to 2oz in April. In June eggs were rationed to one or two per month and clothing rationing began, with an allowance of 66 coupons per person per year. Clothing coupons had to be used for knitting wool, shoes, towels, sheets and blankets, and curtain and dress materials. Men's trousers lost their turnups and pockets on clothes were no longer allowed if unnecessary. Dressing gowns had been made from blankets sometimes, but no longer, and household linens and towels were patched and used until they fell apart. Old towels were made into face flannels, or a square of white lint (not on coupons), hemmed all round made a good facecloth substitute. In October there were oranges for the under-fives, and in November a new 'points' system was introduced for tinned foods, dried fruit and rice. Sixteen points per month each could be spent on any assortment of these goods in any shops, the range of which was increased to include breakfast cereals and biscuits. Sweets and chocolate were in short supply and were later rationed to 3 or 4oz per week.

My father had no previous experience in growing vegetables but planted potatoes and grew beetroot, rhubarb, lettuces, tomatoes and runner beans on the allotment and achieved considerable success. Excess tomatoes were bottled and runner beans salted in large jars for the winter. From February 1940 we enjoyed the extra hour's 'Daylight Saving' throughout the year, which gave welcome extra time in the evening for vegetable growers, and in 1942 a further hour was 'saved' by putting the clocks forward for another hour, so that in the summer dusk began at about 11pm, which made a significant difference to evening activities, and keen 'allotmenteers' toiled until their energy ran out or the light finally failed.

CHAPTER FOURTEEN

Parents' Association – illness strikes – hikes – indoor Campfire –
friends for life – church bell – church parade –
Homologues – The Amber Gate

My father, together with a few interested Scouts' parents, decided to launch a Scouts' and Guides' Parents' Association, and its aim would be to raise money to build a Scout and Guide Hut after the war. There were already two church halls, but the larger of the two had been commandeered by the Gas Company for the duration of the war in which to store gas cookers. The Small Hall, therefore, was where all meetings and social events took place. There was no storage space for equipment and no kitchen facilities, although water heating and a sink were still available in a room off the Large Hall. The logistics of the plan for a Hut were not thought about at the time; it seemed sufficient to provide a purpose for the new Association. My father became the Chairman and planning meetings were held for social evenings in the Small Hall. It was agreed that ladies could bring their knitting, often for Forces comforts, to the meetings.

It was for my fifteenth birthday that I was given a bike. My father had tracked down a second-hand one, tried it out and bought it for me. It was a huge surprise and I was so overjoyed I flung my arms around him in a great hug. That, I think, surprised us both! My social life took me back to St Luke's in the evenings perhaps three or four times in the week, but I had never thought about ever having a bike. There was no outside covered place to keep it; Eric's was still in the aviary, and my father's bike stood in the open by the back gate as he used it every day. To solve the storage problem two boards were placed across the bath and I had to wheel the bike over newspapers if wet and then lift it on to the boards, and off again to use it. It was a heavy bike, but I managed it – of course I did!

In the spring of 1942 my mother fell ill. My father had organised a Parents' Association picnic for the following Sunday and although he was clearly worried about my mother's condition he was adamant that I should go to the picnic as arranged. It took place on Chislehurst Common and I spent a very enjoyable day out with the Scouts and their parents who had become friends. We had a lot of fun and laughter playing Rounders and Cricket and being away from home for the day. I returned home to find that the doctor had visited and had arranged for an ambulance to take my mother to hospital the next day. This was a very frightening blow and I privately shed tears through the shock and apprehension. My father, of course, had to go to work as usual. The ambulance came and I was allowed to accompany my mother to Lewisham Hospital. She was suffering from pneumonia. At the hospital she was put on to a trolley, and with me on a chair by her side, was put into a curtained cubicle where we stayed unattended for several hours. My mother complained of feeling cold, and in the face of hospital authority it took all my courage to waylay and interrupt a busy nurse hurrying past to ask for another blanket, which was provided. Eventually she was found a place in a very crowded ward with beds close together along the sides with no room for visitors chairs between them, and a further row of beds down the centre of the ward.

We did not know it at the time, but her hospital notes read "Dying when admitted". We were told that she was to be treated with some new pills – M and B tablets – which I now learn the Red Cross described then as 'the miracle drug of modern science'. They had previously been reserved for Forces casualties, but were now available for civilians. They must have been penicillin tablets, and no doubt saved her life. After a few weeks my mother recovered sufficiently to be transferred for convalescence to the Joyce Green Hospital near Dartford, a former Isolation Hospital. It was indeed isolated and difficult to reach by public transport. We, my father and I, made weekly Sunday visits, and on those days I would pick all the flowers in bloom in the garden to take with us, as my mother loved flowers and would normally have four or five vases of garden flowers in the living room. The train journey took us to Dartford Station and then a special bus took visitors to the hospital. Two visitors only were allowed at a time, by ticket, which had to be presented. To enable Auntie Flo to visit her sister we had to arrange to meet her outside the hospital to hand over a ticket and wait until she could return it to us before we caught the special bus back to the station. My mother eventually recovered and came home, but had to do arm exercises for a time as her arm muscles had wasted. My father and I coped as best we could while she was away and I had to practice what culinary skills I had acquired. I remember that in an effort to waste nothing I made a large amount of rhubarb jelly, which we even had for breakfast one day to use it up!

There were no Guide camps for us during the war, but as a Patrol Leader I sometimes took my Patrol, the Swallows, on a hike to the campsite. We would meet at Grove Park Station where we would catch a bus to Bromley, and then on to Keston Common, 3d each for them, 6d for me as I was over fourteen. From there we would walk to Downe village and on down the long hill to the campsite. Through the gate we once found the first field, on the side of the valley, had been planted with flax and the flowers were a stunning azure blue and like nothing we had ever seen before. I suppose the eventual seed pods were gathered to make linseed oil. There was a special Hike Field, and to accompany any sandwiches our mothers were able to provide we would light a fire and cook 'dampers'. This mixture of flour with a little dried egg and moistened with water was not curled round a stick and scorched over the fire in true Scout fashion, but cooked flat in a frying pan with a tiny piece of fat and spread with jam if available. We always observed the Guide convention of Rest Hour after lunch, and the sun on the hillside could be quite warm, even in February. I had made myself some footwear which I always changed into for the walk to and from the site. I bought two pairs of thin leather soles which I riveted together, and with pieces of stout blue fabric and cords constructed a pair of very open but tough sandals. I loved the feel of walking through dew-wet grass, and always had dry shoes to change into on the bus home.

My father had always encouraged my practical interests and when he was constructing the nest boxes for his budgies I was allowed to help. At about nine or ten I was sat up to the table with newspapers spread out and shown how to gouge out with a shaped chisel the saucer shape required for the base of the nest, which I happily did to the best of my ability. As a keen Patrol

Leader I wanted now to carve a wooden Patrol Trophy, which I made with my father's tools and his minimal help. It was in the shape of a Guide trefoil badge, with the star shape and G and G letters raised, and the background stippled with the point of a punch. This I stained and varnished and hung on the ceiling lines in the kitchen to dry and I thought it quite splendid. It was about eight inches each way, but the pleasure came in its making, not in its use. As it was difficult to judge which girl to award it to and they were not very good at bringing it back on time to meetings, it was hardly used.

As a senior Patrol Leader I was given the task of bearing the Guide Flag in the Colour Party of three attending the sad funeral of a Guide who had died as a result of burns received when her nightdress ignited when she stood too close to the open fire in her home. We were not required to parade the flag, but just to stand with it at the back of the church to show support. I had not attended a funeral before and found the tears and emotion of the distraught mother following the coffin past us out of the church deeply upsetting. I had not known the Guide very well but naturally we were all saddened by her death.

By that time those of us who were senior Guides had become friendly with the seniors in the Scouts through shared social events. My particular friends included Peter Collins, Peter Kirby and Ron Butler, usually known as 'the two Petes and Ron'. Ron was about my age, we had been in the same infants class at school, although not friends then, and the 'two Petes' were perhaps a year older. At one time we wanted to hold a joint indoor campfire in the Small Hall and the boys constructed a mock fire illuminated by a dim light bulb, which would give a sufficient glow through red tissue paper. Our Guide Captain gave her permission readily, but it fell to me to telephone the Guide District Commissioner, Miss Mabel Grigg, an important person, for her permission to hold this 'mixed activity'. This was the first phone call I had ever made. I explained what we wanted to do and permission was granted – providing we kept the Hall lights on – which of course would spoil the whole effect of a campfire! I cannot remember what we did in the end.

'The Gang's all here!'
Back Row (l to r) – Peter Kirby, George Osmond (Ozzie), Ron Butler, Stan Lee
Front Row – Peter Collins, Roy Hughes, George Ware (Todd).
This was framed on our mantelpiece throughout the war.

My father bought a half-size billiard table which we kept on edge behind the settee in the living room. My Sundays were busy days and after church in the morning, helping at Sunday School in the afternoon and perhaps attending Evensong a little later in the day, the day quietened down until after teatime. Then usually, in ones or twos, enquiring after the others, the trio would arrive and the billiard table would be erected, almost filling the room, and we, with my father, would spend the evening playing snooker and billiards, the 'losers' making the cocoa afterwards. The evenings were full of banter and laughter and ended usually about 11pm. Happy days! If the lads were almost like brothers to me, they were almost like extra sons for my parents for that short while until call-up.

When we had the monthly Church Parade for Scouts and Guides, Cubs and Brownies, we would parade in the street outside in threes and march into the church preceded by the Cross and accompanied by the appropriate flags. We filled most, if not all of the available seating in the Lady Chapel, and a photograph taken in the spring of 1942 shows 110 children and 10 adult leaders on parade. Each colour party of three approached the chancel and presented their flag which was accepted by the officiating priest and stood against the wall by the altar. The service consisted of prayers and hymns, a reading and a short address, and was what today might slightingly be called "a hymn sandwich". The hymns would be well-known from school assemblies, and often also included the hymn for sailors – "Eternal Father, strong to save, whose arm doth bind the restless wave…". At the end of the service we would again file out and the parade would be dismissed. Attendance at Church Parade could not be made compulsory being dependent on the parents' wishes as well as the inclination of the child, but as the enrolment Promise included "…to do my best to do my duty to God…" attendance at Church Parade was presented as a minimal fulfilment of this Promise. I once took it upon myself as a conscientious Patrol Leader to visit a Guide's parents in some trepidation to try to persuade them to ensure that their daughter attended Church Parade. I recall only my feelings of nervousness as the parents' views on the subject were unknown to me.

Church Parade Easter 1942. The Rev Derrick Underwood presides, with Roy Hughes leading with the Cross. Mrs Mayo and Grace lead the Brownies, followed by the Cubs, Guides and Scouts. The roofless church shows the result of the incendiary fire.

In his role as Chairman of the Parents' Association my father was always on the lookout for new fundraising events and dreamed up the idea of giving gramophone record concerts with the stock of records he had amassed and which we often played. He and I made a couple of posters to advertise the concert as a trial effort. Between us we selected a programme of popular music which would have included Gershwin's Rhapsody in Blue, which he had introduced to me years before as a coming classic, one or two operatic Gigli arias, songs by Peter Dawson, a popular tenor of the time, and perhaps orchestral pieces such as lively waltzes and Hungarian dances, Gilbert and Sullivan songs and others. It was an unusual entertainment which was sufficiently supported to merit a further concert.

To celebrate Montgomery's victories in North Africa it was announced that on Wednesday, 11th November 1942 that church bells would be rung all over Britain the following Sunday. St Luke's single bell was still in position, but the bell-rope had burnt away in the incendiary bomb blaze the previous year. It was rumoured, however, that the bell *would* be rung, so we gathered in the roadway outside the church to watch and listen. Soon a ladder appeared and a volunteer climbed to within striking distance of the bell, then producing a large hammer, he slowly struck the bell in a measured way a number of times. We all cheered and applauded this rather bleak and thin sound, but it was the best we could do and we had not heard the bell since September 1939, after which it was only to be rung in case of invasion.

My father introduced another fund-raising idea with his 'Homologue Competition'. The Homologues, I now find should more correctly have been termed Homonyms, pairs of words sounding the same but with different spellings and meanings. Sheets of clues were printed and sold at 6d, with a prize of 5/- for the winner. My father had a way of duplicating writing which, though laborious, was most useful, and I find now that it was called a chromograph. Special purple ink was used to write the script which was then placed face down on a tin tray of jelly, rolled flat and removed. Single sheets were then individually pressed onto the jelly – when taken up they had acquired a readable print and a number of copies could be made. The jelly could be wiped clean and used again. I helped my father with the words for the competition and it was great fun. My father's insurance round had been extended, and knowing all his clients he offered his competition to likely competitors as well as circulating them among the Parents' Association. Any form of local entertainment or diversion from a long war was welcome, and there was no difficulty in selling his Homologue Competition forms. Although there was little to buy in the shops there were constant exhortations to buy Savings Certificates or support the many special collection weeks in aid of aircraft, ships and tanks, but a sixpenny competition was something entertaining to do and puzzle over. My school ran a savings scheme and sold certificates. They bought them in bulk in advance, so that your certificate might be dated several months previous to its purchase, a bonus as the certificates, having gained interest, could be cashed at the end of ten years.

Late in 1942 another senior Scout, Roy Hughes, was called up. He was about two years older than me and lived near to us and his sister Olive was in my Patrol. We knew his parents well and after he was posted abroad to Colombo in Ceylon (now Sri Lanka), they received a telegram from the Admiralty to say that he had been operated on for peritonitis. This was worrying, but was better news than wartime telegrams often brought. I went to see his parents to express our sympathy, but of course there would be no further news until he could send a letter. Several years later Roy told me that in great pain he had had to 'report sick' at the shore station HMS Anderson, and struggling with both his bulky kitbag and hammock, had joined the morning Sick Parade and waited in turn to see the doctor. In hospital the operation to remove his appendix was not entirely successful, and as parts still remained, he had for years to carry a card giving medical detail in case of a sudden recurrence.

When Peter Collins was called up he too was sent to HMS Anderson in Colombo and the three of them, Eric, Roy, and Pete, were able to meet together. Peter Kirby chose the RAF but was compelled to serve as a coalminer for a short time before his RAF training. Ron, the youngest of the three was called-up just after the end of the war and served in Burma with the rank of Sergeant. We all corresponded from time to time but their departures left quite a hole in my life and the occasional letters between us made a very poor substitute for their company. I also wrote to Eric, of course; long screeds about school, activities with the Rangers, news about people in the church, and so on. He entered one of my letters in a ship-board competition for the longest letter by page. He argued that my letter of seventeen foolscap pages should win over a messmate's thirty-five ordinary sized pages from his wife, but to no avail, and Eric had trouble in convincing them that the letter came from his sister!

At St.Luke's during this year we rehearsed for a performance of the play "The Amber Gate". I was never very clear as to what the 'Gate' was, but the production consisted of scenes featuring children or young people famous in history. This gave an ample number of parts for boys and girls and the scenes could be rehearsed separately. Some of the scenes were : Dick Whittington, The Boy who put his finger in the Dyke, The young Handel (with his candle!), and The Young George Washington. I was asked to be Mrs. Washington, an undemanding part. There were also songs to be rehearsed, to the near despair of our elderly organist, Mr. Lambert the father of our Guide Lieutenant, as we were not always very cooperative. The rehearsals were enormous fun and an excuse for all of us to be together, but I'm not sure whether we ever produced the play or whether wartime difficulties precluded it. When we rehearsed in the Community Centre my mother brought Binkie to be Dick Whittington's cat, but though normally docile, he ran away. He had obviously no ambition to "tread the boards"!

CHAPTER FIFTEEN

School Certificate – the Fun Fair – Prefect – Rangers – "Fire!"

I sat for the School Certificate exams in 1943 and was late at school for one of them as the air raid siren had sounded within five minutes of my leaving home. I knocked on the door of the nearest house and sat out the raid, which did not appear to be near us, in their shelter, before continuing to school. As I was late I tore up the nearest stairs from the Library, which were normally forbidden to us. It was agreed to let me sit the exam, but on my own, downstairs, in the Library.

When the results of the exams were read out at Prayers one day the Headmistress read the names and often said, after the name, "Matriculation Exemption". I had no idea what that was and again felt that void in my knowledge of the academic world. We were told that although I had gained the certificate it was not of a sufficient standard for the continuation of my scholarship, but I could redeem it by sitting for the Supplementary School Certificate in a few subjects the following year. This was agreed. I had achieved the Pass mark in six subjects, English, English Literature, History (English and European), Elementary Maths, and Art, with a Very Good (the highest standard) in French, written and oral. The one subject in which I failed was Geography, the teaching of which for me, left much to be desired, but I nevertheless apologised to the

Geography mistress for my failure. I was conscious in class that my printing of names on maps was irregular and uneven, and tried to improve by taking all my notes in the lessons in fast capital letters in the vain hope of reaching a more regular style. Geography lessons seemed mainly to consist of personal amusing anecdotes from the teacher who often brought in the phrase "… the friend with whom I live…" There were a few 'crushes' on one or two members of staff that year and Miss Laidler, who taught Geography, was one who inspired these painful passions, but not in me. I had struggled with the homework in a fog of difficulty, as when I was required to draw on a map of Britain the position of the coalfields. As the map provided was little bigger than a postage stamp I was reduced to making a few hopeful blobs on the top half of the map.

In the spring of 1943 the Parents' Association had agreed an ambitious plan to hold a fund-raising Fun Fair in June. There was a useful strip of ground alongside the church but it was covered in the ash and the burnt remains of the roof of the nave of the church although the large roof beams had been removed. The Church Council gave their permission for the Fun Fair provided that we cleared the site first ourselves. This was a dirty, dusty and heavy job which was achieved with aid of the older Scouts, the parents, and the trek cart, after church on Sunday mornings. Most Scout troops owned a trek cart and their dimensions varied according to the materials available. The basic construction was an open-topped shallow box, possibly measuring about 4 feet by 3 feet and about 12 inches deep, but these measurements were not in any way standard. The cart was propelled by two large wheels about 3 feet in diameter fixed halfway along the sides and steered by a long shaft of about 4 feet with a short cross-piece at the end. Two scouts stood behind the cross-piece to push it, which pulled the cart along, aided by others pushing at the back. It was used to take equipment to camp and to provide transport for a great range of tasks that the Scouts performed, including salvage collections during the war, and help with furniture salvage from bombsites.

Scouts, on the trek cart, publicising the Fun Fair, June 12th 1943. Colour, noise, spectacle, fun and games!

The trek cart was again used on the 12th June to publicise the Fun Fair to be held at St Luke's two days later. The weather was fine and sunny and every Scout who could dress up in a costume, sport a funny hat, beard or make-up piled in or helped pull the cart around the streets to make the event known, with much noise and laughter. By great good fortune the 14th June was also sunny, although most of the eighty or so children in the photo are wearing coats. From early morning we were at the site, putting up tables borrowed from the Small Hall for the stalls, or roping off areas for hoopla, and so on. Fortunately the grass had grown again since the fire in 1941, and was by now fairly level. The Parents' Association and Scouts had made great efforts to unearth, invent, or borrow games and competitions, and these were installed on tables and sites to their best advantage. Our train set was pressed into service and a circular track was laid out on two trestle tables and various railway stations were denoted around the edge. When all the tickets had been sold, the train was wound up and ran around the track to stop randomly at or near a winning station.

Excitement mounted as children and some parents queued to enter when all was ready after a brief lunch. Admission was by the production of two or three jam jars or a few pence. The jam jars were temporarily stored in the outside porch of the church, which occasioned a few grumbles later from the congregation elders. The noise level rose as the stallholders vied for customers and cheers went up for the winners.

We were not allowed to give money prizes, and the usual toys, sweets and small ornaments for fairground use were not available in wartime, but my father once again solved the problem. He had learnt how to use the treadle sewing machine years earlier when he machined together long strips of red and green crepe paper which, twisted, made Christmas paper chain decorations. This time he used the machine to perforate rows of token tickets which he had printed on the jelly duplicator. These were torn off and given as prizes and could be exchanged for sixpenny savings stamps at our garden shelter which became the seat of exchange. This was my department for the afternoon. My father, as chief organiser, money changer and recipient of the stalls' takings, was on duty throughout and wore a gold paper crown for quick identification. Kind donations from parents of carefully-saved spoonfuls of tea and sugar provided a cup of tea each for the adult stallholders during the afternoon and was much appreciated.

The Fun Fair, run mainly, of course, for children, was a huge success and great fun for us all, providing not only a fund-raising event but also a local outdoor entertainment. My father would have been amazed if anyone had suggested that all his efforts in this were a contribution to the 'war effort' in keeping up civilian morale!

The fun fair at its height. My father in his gold crown is just visible near the centre where the crowd is watching the Train Game.

The 'admission fee' jam-jars were later taken to our garden and added to the collection the Scouts normally made from around the streets. The jars were washed in large zinc baths on the lawn if necessary and stored in the now empty aviary, my father's birds having long gone owing to the lack of imported birdseed. When sufficient jars had been collected they were taken by trek cart down the long hill to Robertson's jam factory with its golliwog advertisement outside. The factory paid a ha'penny for one pound jars and 1d for two pound jars. It does not sound as though the gain was worth all the effort, but it was a way of raising money without any outlay in expenses and all avenues had to be explored. It was also a means for the Scouts to contribute to the War Effort by salvaging the jars.

It had been decided that I would take English, English Literature and Art for the Supplementary School Certificate, and subject to satisfactory results would go on to the Secretarial Sixth Form and take a one-year course in those skills. This course could be for one or two years, and I imagine the two-year students received better results and higher speeds in shorthand and typing.

At some time I received one interview regarding careers, probably just before the School Certificate exams. As I did not want either to teach or to train as a nurse the interviewer seemed rather at a loss as to what to suggest. Horticulture was diffidently proposed, but it still seemed as though I would need to go to college. To be quite honest, I was scared and apprehensive at the prospect of living away from home, being conscious of how much I did not know about the world, academic and social, and how it worked. So I fudged the situation, pretending I thought my sight would not stand up to a lot of close study, and that ended the interview.

Some of us were made Prefects for these final two years. It was not a very onerous appointment. We were expected generally to keep an eye on behaviour in the cloakroom, but we had no specific responsibilities towards individual Forms. Apart from not allowing talking as girls waited in line outside classrooms before a lesson began, our main duty, taken in rotation, was to stand at the top of the flight of stairs to the first floor to supervise the flow up and down the stairs between lessons and the beginning and end of the day. "No talking" and "Single file" were to be maintained both ways. Vigilance and a strong voice were all that was needed to keep order.

Before Prayers each morning it was the senior Prefect's duty to obtain from the Headmistress in her room the hymnbook and papers needed and to walk the length of the Hall and to place them on the lectern on the platform. A few minutes later the Headmistress would make the same journey and the Assembly would begin. Some Head Prefects found this a nerve-wracking experience every day, but others would sail through it easily. Because of various absences I found myself having to do this duty once, and I think I could have got used to it. Our Form Mistress for these two years was little Miss Ridge who had probably been brought out of retirement. She had previously taught French, we understood. She was obviously out of her depth with this crowd of large opinionated girls. We took some pride, and status we thought, in being the last form who had been at the Prendergast School for a year before the war, as though everyone else were alien newcomers! Poor Miss Ridge became clearly terrified when those of us who were Prefects threatened to resign and turn in our badges over some perceived slight or dispute. She barely kept a hold on us.

By the autumn as I was sixteen I was no longer a Guide but had moved on to the senior branch, Rangers. We were given the task of ringing the church bell during the Communion Service on Sunday mornings. Two of us had to slip out of our seats during the service, one to listen and watch for the appropriate time, the raising of the Host, and to signal to the bell-ringer who had balanced along a single plank laid over the ruined floor of the church, to the base of the bell-tower. The bell-rope had been replaced and it took some skill to work out the correct timing of the three rings required. It was a source of some pride and satisfaction when this was perfectly performed and I hope enhanced the worship. We no longer wore the 'Guide blue' uniforms but now needed pale grey jumpers for the winter and a pale grey fine poplin blouse for the summer, both worn with a navy skirt. There were only a handful of us and activities were very restricted. An attempt was made to treat us more as adults when we learnt how to use a stirrup pump properly to put out fires. There was also an occasion when we arrived on our meeting night to find the Small Hall full of smoke, with the assurance that people inside needed rescuing! Our efforts at this, keeping everyone as near the floor as possible while dragging the inert victims out were not hugely successful, but we probably learnt something, and the victims survived. The dustbin inside with its smouldering hay had to be quickly extinguished before the neighbours became alarmed by the smoke and called the Fire Brigade!

CHAPTER SIXTEEN

Art and English – Ottershaw holiday – mystery explosion –
outdoor Shakespeare – new shoes – Prisoners of War

In September 1943 I joined the Sixth Form group who were starting the two-year Higher School Certificate course, but my subjects were only English Language and English Literature. For my third subject for the Supplementary exam, Art, I completed various projects in the Art Room including a large river and trees scene in pen and ink. It was subsequently displayed on the wall in the Art Room with a caption "After Van Gogh" without my permission, which annoyed me intensely. The books I had studied to learn the technique and to draw the trees and plot the scene had nothing to do with Van Gogh, but any protests from me would probably have been regarded as querying the Art mistress's authority so I could only grumble to my friends.

We had an excellent English teacher that year, Miss Acheson. She seemed elderly and was probably just over retirement age. She wore rather old-fashioned soft creamy blouses with droopy chains or necklaces and her pale auburn hair seemed often at the point of falling down from where she had pinned it up. Out of fashion she may have been, but not so much as our Religious Instruction teacher in 1938 who wore her hair in two tight meagre plaits curled like earphones on her ears! Through Miss

Acheson we were introduced to the romantic poets, Tennyson, Keats, Browning, Matthew Arnold, etc. We explored their verses and techniques in detail, and Miss Acheson would occasionally read a poem to us which brought it to life. One such poem was Tennyson's Œnone, the only line which I remember, often repeated was "Dear mother Ida, hearken 'ere I die!" It brought some of us near to tears, even 'Pussy' Wenmouth. Her real name was Astrid and she usually sat silent and unresponsive during lessons, like a 'pussy-cat', as a member of staff had said in frustration. Miss Acheson's teaching and my own love of the subject produced the results I needed. When the results came through I had gained Very Good in English, and Credits (midway between Very Good and Pass) in English Literature and Art, to add to my Very Good in French.

We were very grateful for a week's holiday in the early summer of 1944; our first holiday for five years, at Pottery Cottage – the home in Ottershaw, Surrey, of my father's Aunt Nan and Uncle Fred Pooley. It was a very relaxing holiday, although the adults spent hours chatting, particularly at meal times, tying me to the table too. I was too old to ask "Please may I get down", but the talk seemed always to be about relatives and times I did not remember!

My father and I were loaned fishing rods and lines and spent most of our mornings fishing in a nearby stream. Unfortunately, through an unlucky cast of a line, the top segment of a rod caught in a tree and fell into the stream. Although we searched and waded in the water for some time we could not find the missing piece and felt very guilty and apologetic on our return to the cottage.

Market Day in Guildford was on a Tuesday and we travelled there by bus, a very pleasant ride. I bought a poster showing the new Cathedral, then only partly built, as it would be when finished; it had been hailed as very modern in design and very different from traditional styles. The poster stayed on my bedroom wall, because I liked it, for years. All good things come to an end, and on the train journey home we could see occasional smoke plumes that reminded us we were returning to London, air raids, and our usual war-time life.

Not many days after our return came the tremendous news of the invasion of Europe – D Day. I heard the news on the wireless as I was ironing in the living room. We had no ironing board, but used a thick blanket and sheet on the unpolished dining table. The electric iron was connected to the light fitting over the table by a two-way plug. The first announcements were necessarily brief, but it was clear that an enormous action was taking place which would bring the end of the war closer. It was impossible for us to comprehend the scale of the operation at the time and the extent of the battle lines. Soon after the war began my father had pinned up a Daily Telegraph map of Europe with the idea of plotting the progress of the war, but I do not think he did very much with it as the situation in France and the Netherlands at first was of retreats. The map may have vanished from the wall before the Normandy landings in 1944, which would have provided events worth plotting.

A little later in the month when the air raid siren had sounded one evening, my mother and I went down to the shelter, but my father was on duty that night at the Wardens' Post at the Community Centre nearby. Soon after midnight we heard aircraft noise and then a tremendous crash or explosion very near to us. We heard shrapnel and debris falling all around us in the garden, and then the thunder of boots as the Wardens came tearing down the road. Something, a plane or a bomb, had come down in the allotments about fifty yards away. There was a large crater and as its cause could not be clearly seen in the dark the Wardens left someone on guard for the rest of the night, to deter spectators and the curious. We climbed out of the shelter after little sleep to find at 5am pieces of roof tile all over the garden, and the roof looked as though it had been stirred up with a stick. The blast had also blown in the glass of the kitchen windows and the back door off its hinges which in falling had cut my mother's shopping basket neatly in two. It took the three of us until 7 o'clock before we had cleared up all the glass and made the kitchen habitable again. Instead of our usual cereals we had baked beans on toast for breakfast! We were tired and hungry and reckoned we had earned it.

It was not until my mother washed the kitchen curtains a few weeks later that she found they had sustained numerous small unrepairable cuts from the shattered windows and were unusable. Some neighbours had claimed War Damage Reparation immediately for their curtains and other items but as the curtains were not obviously torn at the time, my parents felt it would be dishonest to claim for them. It was now too late to enter a claim, so new material had to be bought using our precious clothing coupons.

With new information it was soon established by the Wardens that the crater had been caused by one of the first V1 rockets. We soon learned to watch the Doodlebugs, or Buzz bombs as they were called to denigrate them with silly names, and to estimate by their direction and their position when the engine cut out and the rocket began to fall, whether we were in danger.

It had been arranged by the school that the Sixth Form could attend an outdoor performance of 'The Merchant of

Venice' at a house in Beckenham that same afternoon, and my parents insisted that in spite of the clearing up still to be done at home, I should take this unique opportunity to see a Shakespeare play performed by live actors. The actors, it is true, were amateur and had to be found among either the too young, or those unfitted or too old for military service. We thought the two courtiers, Salario and Salarino, were played by local schoolboys aged about sixteen – no older than ourselves! It was a brilliantly sunny afternoon and we sat enthralled on chairs on the lawn of a large house which had two grassy terraces making an excellent stage. We drank in every minute and word of the performance, and starved as we were of cultural experiences, we were thrilled and appreciative of this splendid theatrical offering, and reluctantly came 'back down to earth' and life in our very different century, at the play's ending.

The military side of the war was proceeding encouragingly but civilian life remained much the same with strict food rationing and a shortage of goods in the shops with little choice. All fabrics, clothes, shoes and knitting wool were available only by surrendering the appropriate number of 'clothing coupons', and sale articles were almost a thing of the past. My mother had made sets of summer pyjamas for me just before the war on the style of the 'beach pyjamas' then in vogue. The top was collarless with short sleeves in a tunic style, and with an embroidered V on the pocket, and the trousers had the very wide legs so much in fashion then. They were made in a soft rayon fabric and my mother was always careful on wash days never to subject them to the harsh wooden rollers of the mangle, preferring to wring them by hand, to avoid breaking the threads of this lightweight fabric. Her care allowed me to wear these much-loved pyjamas every summer through to the late 40's. Although my father did not need to dress quite so smartly as an Insurance Agent, his clothes were given fairly hard treatment by his daily round on his bike. My mother still spent much time in re-furbishing his shirts, not so much then for economic reasons, but simply because clothing coupons had to be carefully hoarded and used to the best advantage only when absolutely necessary. Dresses for my mother and I were seldom made, and I have no memories of any enthusiasm for new styles or colours.

Although school uniform was still preferred, we were allowed in the upper forms now to wear navy skirts instead of the tunics. The paper dress patterns and styles in the pattern books were either for children's clothes or adults; there were no 'in-between' styles for girls in their teenage years and it was difficult to reconcile one's fancies with the sober adult designs on one hand or the childish patterns on the other, but my mother did her very best for me. One day we arranged to meet after school to buy me a new pair of shoes, but a shortage of styles and an unhelpful assistant seemed likely to turn our quest into failure. The assistant persisted in offering me one-bar clumpy child's shoes to try on. This was probably because I had small feet and was wearing school uniform, but my mother, trying to do better for me, cried out "She may take a small size, but she's *seventeen!*". This had some effect and we did finally manage to buy a more adult pair of shoes. Shoes were now becoming fashion items for us in the Sixth Form, and wedge heels began to appear but of course shoes could only be bought by using clothing coupons. We were envious one day when Dottie (Dorothy) Hardstone, sporting new 'wedgies', mentioned she had sisters younger than herself and had been able to acquire a few extra coupons! The rest of our little group of friends, Joan Elllis, Gwen Sextone and Valda Smart had no such advantages.

It must have been later that year when a hut was erected on the allotment site near to the main entrance alongside our garden. Italian Prisoners of War were brought there daily to start digging foundations for the Prefabricated houses that were to be erected all over the field no longer scheduled to become a park. No one seemed to be bothered by this; we seldom saw them and they made no alteration in our lives. The neighbour whose house was the closest to the prisoners gave them a guitar that her son no longer used, to provide them with some entertainment. My parents did not discuss the prisoners or the situation regarding the war in my hearing, and my mother was not a gossip. She had made a friend, however, with a Mrs Keir who had moved into our little block with her husband. They had had two sons in the Navy, one of whom had been killed on active service, and the Navy connection between them made a friendly bond.

The V1 Doodlebugs continued to arrive throughout the summer but luckily no more fell very near to us. My Ranger friends and I had had our services offered to a local Rest Centre and we volunteered to help in any way we could. On the only occasion when I was asked to help all I did was to sit beside a little girl in bed. I was not told of the circumstances that had brought her there, and she seemed too sleepy to need me to talk to her. My father mistakenly thought I might have seen some tragic casualties and asked me not to tell my mother about them as he did not want her to be upset. I did not tell him how useless I had felt.

In September the rumoured V2 rockets, unmanned with 2000 pounds of explosives began to make their deadly unheralded attacks.

CHAPTER SEVENTEEN

The V2 rocket – Secretarial Sixth – holiday at Pottery Cottage –
the cultural desert – Exam results – VJ Day – starting work

Although the end of the war was forecast, the Doodlebugs and terrifying V2 rockets continued to harry the civilian population. On the 23rd January 1945 I had left the kitchen after breakfast for a last visit to the bathroom before leaving the house to catch the bus for school. There was suddenly a tremendous explosion and reverberating noise followed immediately by my father's voice calling my name urgently and distractedly. A V2 rocket had landed in the Hither Green Cemetery about 120 yards away. The force of the blast had blown open our front door and my father rushed into the road, thinking I had been blown out into the street. In fact I was still in the bathroom, mopping myself up, as the power of the explosion had caused a huge surge of water in the underground pipes, up into the lavatory *just* as I was about to use it. Still rather damp, I called out to my distraught father. The rocket had landed close to Verdant Lane and large canvas screens were hastily erected along the edge of the cemetery and the gardens of the houses opposite while work began to clear the road of debris and body remains from the graves – a grisly job. I had to take an alternative route to school that day as Verdant Lane had to be closed.

I had now been for one term in the Secretarial Sixth Form. We used a large room, formerly the Dining Room on the first floor, which was equipped with long tables in rows bearing our typewriters. We sat side by side while Mrs James, our teacher, set us tests, taught us shorthand, and timed our speeds with her stopwatch. In other classrooms we also learnt a smattering of commercial French, and some of the basics of Spanish, as well as very elementary bookkeeping. It cannot have been easy with the class at two levels, beginners, and those who had already had one year's tuition. We were watched over by a large print of 'The Girl with the Pearl Earring', although I did not know its title then. Outside in the corridor there was a print entitled 'The Doge of Venice', a very impressive man, and these two pictures if explained, could have been a lesson in themselves, but it was probably thought more important to stick to the syllabus for all the impending examinations. My year in the Secretarial Sixth of necessity largely separated me from my two best friends, Joan Ellis and Gwen Sexstone, who had spent a weekend with us after her home had been badly damaged in an air raid. They were both continuing to work for the Higher School Certificate with the aim of qualifying for a Teacher's Training Course at a college.

Polyfotos, in differing poses in sheets of about 20, became all the rage

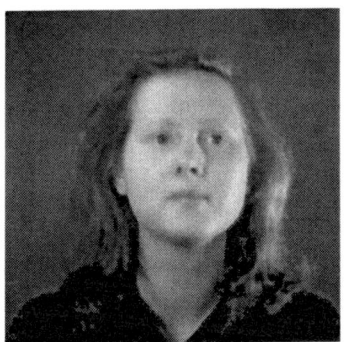

Some of my school friends – a) Joan Ellis, b) Christine Risley, c) Eileen Orchard

Away from friends at school, I missed the fun, friendship and busyness of the preceding few teenage years. There seemed to be little of my former enjoyable social life left. Ron Butler and I were, of course, still firm friends and we often went to the cinema on Saturday evenings in Bromley and enjoyed the long walk home, talking all the way. There still may have been the occasional 'Socials' in the Small Hall, but none stay in my memory.

After church on Sunday mornings, I would often find myself alone in the living room with hand sewing, clothes-repairing jobs to be done, and to raise my spirits in my low spells I devised a programme of gramophone records, always played in the same order. The Overture to 'Poet and Peasant' with its strong, noisy orchestral rhythms caught my gloomy mood and this was followed by one or two of Chopin's Etudes, 'Consolation' being one. My choices were, of course, limited to the selection of records we had acquired in the Keith Prowse days, and the next choice was Gigli, singing 'Your tiny hand is frozen' from La Boheme. His rich emotional style and soaring voice bridged the gap to the next record which was, I think, the Rhapsody in Blue by Gershwin. Even now, if I hear it played I can almost subconsciously note the point at which one side of the record came to an end and it needed to be turned over and the gramophone rewound. Further titles are lost to me now, but I know that a lively Hungarian Dance or Rhapsody with its cheerful energetic melody completed my 'cure for the blues'.

It was not easy to make the transition into young adulthood amid the constrictions of wartime shortages and social deprivations. Some of us still wore white blouses and navy skirts, cardigans, raincoats, and velour or panama hats, but when these were outgrown we were allowed to wear our own dresses and my friend Joan Ellis also sported a stylish, stiff white raincoat. There were very few role models for us to emulate. Glamorous film stars such as Veronica Lake, with a fall of hair half-obscuring her face could not really be copied at school, and radio and film personalities such as 'Gert and Daisy' clad in pinafores were no help either. Perhaps I was particularly short of assistance and advice to bridge the gap between child and adult because I had no older sisters or stylish female friends or relatives; my aunts were mostly away at Reading and in their thirties anyway. I had not realised that my mother was an older woman until Joan Ellis mentioned it was her mother's thirty-eighth birthday. I had been born when my mother was thirty-five, and she was fifty-three by 1945, and of no real help in ushering me into near adult fashion and society. We were beginning to experiment with make-up, and I overheard a derisive remark by a friend after I must have mentioned with regard to face powder, that I used 'a mixture of Pond's and Icilma'. This was to create the colour I wanted, but was obviously not acceptable among the more sophisticated. Once more I felt I was one step behind my contemporaries. I wonder what make of face-powder *was* acceptable?

Most of my form seemed to be in their second year in the Secretarial Sixth, and I made friends with Eileen Orchard who sat next to me. I sometimes found it easier to read Eileen's shorthand than my own! It was at Eileen's suggestion early in 1946 that I applied to fill a vacancy in the Registrar's Office in

University College London, where she had worked since leaving school. In spite of confusing University College with the Senate House of London University in the same street, I arrived only a little late for the interview with Miss Gregg and was accepted. I had felt the time was right to move on from my first job as there was very little opportunity for me to use the skills I had acquired in shorthand and typing. I thoroughly enjoyed my time in the Registrar's Office, even coping with the vast backlog of filing brought back from the College's evacuation as I found it an interesting challenge to track down and attach further letters and information to the appropriate students' files for the preceding war years.

The Registrar was a kindly, old-fashioned and somewhat eccentric gentleman, who brought his pet slow worm to be looked after in the Zoology Department when he went on holiday! The office was run by his secretary Miss Lily Cooper, who could be rather unbending at times to her two juniors. Eileen, rather more qualified and ambitious than I, soon left to join ICI, an important chemical organisation. In the office we dealt with applications from prospective students either by post or in person at the counter. They, or sometimes their parents on their behalf, would bring their examination certificates and seek help in completing the admission application form. There were also students who called in almost every day for news about their grants under the Government Further Education and Training Scheme for ex-service personnel. When a vacancy occurred I applied and was accepted for the twin posts of Clerk to the Faculty of Arts and Secretary to the Tutor to Arts Students, a classicist, Dr McLellan.

But all this was in the future, and first we had to pass our Royal Society of Arts examinations after our somewhat intensive course in shorthand and typing together with basic skills in the other subjects. None of these subjects lent themselves to homework, and Mrs James worked hard to raise our speeds in typing and shorthand which were most important if we were going to find jobs on leaving school.

Once again we were invited to spend a week's holiday at Pottery Cottage with Aunt Nan, Uncle Fred and Harry in early May. We were again offered rods and lines for fishing and my father and I spent happy sunny mornings in the peace and quiet of the riverbank nearby. It was very restful and although we had only a little bread paste for bait we enjoyed watching the floats for possible bites. All we caught were gudgeon, small sprat-like fish which tasted rather muddy when cooked, as all river fish seemed to.

One of the great treats for me during our holidays at Pottery Cottage were the visits to Addlestone where in 1944 I bought a copy of Palgrave's Golden Treasury of poetry and a book of Robert Browning's poems, and in 1945, copies of Matthew Arnold's poems and the Third Series of 'Poems for Today'.

Although I did not realise it at the time the disadvantages of living in the suburbs during the war were made manifest in a variety of ways. Isolated on the Council Estate on the 'green fields of Downham', we were in neither a village nor a town. There was no central structure as there would have been in a village, nor were the amenities of the culture and sophistication of a town available to us. St Luke's church was the nearest to a hub in our community, but the differing styles and personalities of a succession of priests-in-charge, and the small size of the congregation made for constant changes in procedure and stability. In a village there would have been a Parish Council or committee to organise, for example, campaigns to popularize and support the necessary Savings Weeks or initiatives by the Women's Institute or Women's Voluntary Services, which had no representation in our estate. The youth organisations would have been more connected to their District and County projects and aims too, with encouragement to be a part of national war efforts such as salvage collection, and perhaps the Scouts would have served as messengers for the Air Raid Wardens. We had no local Home Guard and there would have been very few able men to make up a local unit. Had we lived in a town there would have been the possibility of a few cultural events such as concerts, choirs, and amateur dramatics. There would also have been a greater variety of shops. But Catford and Lewisham were cultural deserts at that time. The churches each had their own communities and organisations, with 'Savings Thermometers' and posters advertising their activities. In Catford, a St Laurence's Church poster once read "If your knees knock — kneel on them!" The Town Hall may have put on the occasional show or concert, but we were not near enough to appreciate them: a double journey in the blackout by public transport was not to be embarked upon unless by necessity. There were no bookshops in Rushey Green, on either side of the road, which was entirely taken up with food and clothing shops, Woolworths and a chemist.

Suddenly, during our holiday at Pottery Cottage, Germany surrendered and VE Day was declared. In an isolated bungalow in the country all we could do in celebration was to light a small bonfire. The ages of my relatives precluded any idea of rushing into the nearest town to join in the festivities. On a bus in Addlestone the next day I heard everyone talking excitedly about the 'End of the War', but for us it was not over: Eric, Roy, and Pete C. and others were still serving in the Far East on ships and shore. The end of *their* war was to be delayed until August and one at a time they returned home that autumn; the longest-serving, Eric and then Roy Hughes, were repatriated first, soon followed by Peter Collins.

Preparations were now beginning for the General Election which was to take place in July. Banners were stretched across our street, all bearing the same injunction – "Vote Labour". To me, knowing nothing about politics, the rejection of Winston Churchill seemed a very poor return for all the dedication and leadership he had shown since 1940.

We sat for all of our various examinations and our examining board was mainly the Royal Society for the Encouragement of Arts, Manufactures and Commerce London. I gained Credits in both Typewriting and Bookkeeping, a Certificate of the Second Class in French, a Certificate in Shorthand for 60 words per minute, and also a London Chamber of Commerce Elementary Certificate, with Distinction, for the same Shorthand speed. The end of the term drew near and we prepared to leave the school which had educated us to the best of its ability through almost seven years, with evacuation, staffing and equipment shortages, and the inevitable eroding of pre-war standards. Our last morning's Prayers was an emotional occasion as we sang, and realised the words now applied to us – "Lord, dismiss us with Thy blessing, All who here shall meet no more ——", and there were quite a few damp hankies and sniffles at the back of the Hall as we prepared to file out for the last time.

Subject to their results at the Higher School Certificate Examination, my friends would be going to various colleges, and many of us in the Secretarial Sixth had been found jobs through connections maintained over the years by our indefatigable Mrs James. She had found a place for me as a shorthand typist at the Workers' Educational Association's Head Office in Pimlico. My parents seemed to accept this as suitable, no doubt once more putting their trust in the school's authority.

The summer ground on until the news of the atom bombing of Japan broke violently upon us. We had seen the pictures on the cinema screen of the relief of the concentration camps and all the horror they showed, and now the laying waste of Hiroshima was too terrible to be properly taken in. Just as for fifty years or more after the war, the sound of air raid sirens on radio, cinema or television would give me a roiling-surge sensation in the pit of my stomach, so a photo of that mushrooming cloud foretelling such appalling devastation in Japan would bring about an inner cold dread, even sixty years later.

Between the bombing of Japan and its final surrender people had begun to build bonfires in anticipation. We watched as more and more wood was piled up on the spare ground next to our house. On the evening of VJ Day Ron Butler called in to see us. He was the only one left at home of my three close friends and was awaiting call-up. We thought we would go and look at the celebrations in the streets around us, but we did not find other people's celebrations particularly interesting to watch, so we returned to find the Castillon Road bonfire well and truly alight and blazing to the sky. It seemed dangerously close and the side wall of our house became rather too warm to the touch. Again we did not really feel part of the street's celebrations and joined my parents indoors and listened to the news reports on the wireless of celebrations in Trafalgar Square and outside the Palace. After all the anticipation we all felt rather flat.

Within a very short space of time I left my sheltered nest of school, home and church, and like the moorhen chicks on the pond at Shirley Dene, fell headlong into the big world to sink or swim. There had been no reason for me to travel to London during the preceding years and for the first time I saw through the grimy train windows the actual devastation caused by the Blitz and subsequent bombs and rockets. Empty spaces, gaunt walls showing gaps where windows had been blown out, wrecked buildings which although shattered were not in danger of collapse; all these became commonplace sights during my journeys to and from work for years.

After the end of the war — my father and mother

After the end of the war – Eric and I

For the time that I was at the WEA my shorthand and typing skills were hardly used, and the fortuitous move to University College London in 1946 began a progressive period through promotion and marriage, until the end of 1951 when I left full-time paid employment to become a full-time housewife. But meanwhile, still at the WEA that first autumn, a colleague at the end of a day looked out of the window down into the dark street. "There's a sailor down there", she said, "Standing by the lamp-post. Is he waiting for you?" "Yes", I replied, smiling happily, "I rather think he is!"